Other Books by Roger Fritz

What Managers Need to Know

Productivity and Results

Performance Based Management

Rate Yourself as a Manager

You're in Charge: A Guide for Business and Personal Success

The Inside Advantage

Nobody Gets Rich Working for Somebody Else

Personal Performance Contracts

If They Can—You Can! Lessons from America's New Breed of Successful Entrepreneurs

Rate Your Executive Potential

Management Ideas That Work

How to Export: Everything You Need to Know to Get Started

Ready, Aim, HIRE! (Co-author)

The Entrepreneurial Family: How to Sustain the Vision and Value in Your Family Business

Family Ties and Business Binds: How to Solve the Inevitable Problems of Family Businesses

Think Like a Manager

Sleep Disorders: America's Hidden Nightmare

Sales Manager's High Performance Guide: The Only Reference You Need to Build a Powerful Sales Force

A Team of Eagles

How to Manage Your Boss

The Small Business Troubleshooter

Wars of Succession

Fast Track: How To Gain and Keep Momentum

One Step Ahead: The Unused Keys to Success

Bounce Back and Win: What It Takes and How To Do It

Magnet People: Their Secrets and How To Learn From Them

Little Things—Big Results: How Small Events Determine Our Fate

How to Make Your Boss Your Ally and Advocate

Building Your Legacy: One Decision At a Time

100 Ways to Bring Out Your Best

ON CD-ROM

The Personal Business Coach

Beyond Commitment: The Skills All Leaders Need

— *After* —
— *You* —

**Can Humble
People Prevail?**

The least obvious
leadership trait
is *humility*.

— *After* —
— *You* —

Can Humble
People Prevail?

Roger Fritz

Inside Advantage Publications
Naperville, Illinois

Published by:
Inside Advantage Publications
1240 Iroquois Drive, Suite 406
Naperville, IL 60563
Phone: 630-420-7673
Fax: 630-420-7835
rfritz3800@aol.com
http:://www.rogerfritz.com

Unless specifically noted by naming others, all quotations are attributable to the author, Roger Fritz.

Cover and Book Design by Charles King
This book was typeset with Adobe® In Design®.

1-893987-25-6

http://www.rogerfritz.com

Inside Advantage Publications
Naperville, Illinois

Reprinted Network Leadership South Africa (Pty) Ltd
P O Box 13541, Mowbray, 7705

To the memory of

Dr. Robert K. Burns

*Founder of the Industrial Relations Center
at the University of Chicago.*

*My mentor and friend whose work lives
on in countless places because of his
creative ideas, humility and never-ending
compulsion to be helpful.*

Long gone, but never forgotten.

Acknowledgments

I am especially grateful for the ideas and skills of these people: **Tom Heimsoth**, **Larry Olson** and **Gene French** for their insights in evaluating draft manuscripts.

Irene O'Neill for her patience and keeping me on track through many revisions.

Patty Keenan for careful editing.

Charles King for his creative design work.

Contents

Introduction

I know what you're thinking. Is this guy serious? If so, he surely hasn't been anywhere near my world.

My objective is not to try to disprove what you have seen but to suggest new ways to interpret it. "Me First" behavior is undeniable. Its significance lies in the impact upon those affected. I believe that impact is bad and getting worse because most of us haven't really tried to understand what we can do to become an *After You* person.

My hope is that the concepts and examples in this book will help you examine the key requirements of an *After You* outlook and anticipate the likely results.

The least obvious leadership trait is humility. The test? Look around. Observe the behavior of those who are in leadership positions but not doing well. What do they have in common? Almost always, it is behavior that *assumes* you will take them more seriously if they act superior. The assumption is that if they act like their needs, interests and desires are more important than yours, you will defer to them. That you will always accept their whims and preferences. They are **very, very** wrong!

The truth is, we want to follow people who *really* understand us. We look for those who do not push us aside as they chase their own ambitions and vanity. Leaders who survive the test of time don't just talk about better days, they help us achieve them.

1

Why Arrogance Is Vulnerable

> None are so empty
> as those who are full of
> themselves.
>
> —Andrew Jackson,
> seventh U.S. President

Arrogant people can't see beyond themselves. A craving to satisfy only their own desires keeps them constantly focused inward. They are vulnerable because they refuse to acknowledge their weaknesses and do not understand how to gain and keep the support they need from others. Their weak attempts to show that they care about anyone but themselves are transparent and usually backfire.

No one wants to buffer for them. It is easy to let them be exposed to situations where they are likely to fail. No one steps forward to help or defend them. The underlying attitude toward arrogant people when trouble arises is, "let's see how they handle this by themselves," or "they don't believe anyone else is needed, here's their chance to prove it."

The career of General George C. Marshall is a great example of the benefits of self-examination and staying out of the spotlight. Discouraged by being passed over for promotion several times, he came to realize that his quick temper was holding him back. He stopped flaring and concentrated on remaining calm.

As he advanced in rank, he backed off to let superior officers conduct press conferences while he worked in the background. He deliberately selected staff people whose views were different than his own in order to ensure that all sides of issues were examined.

By 1943, his reputation for thorough decision-making was so strong, President Franklin Roosevelt chose him to be Army chief of Staff and a 5-star General. He later served as Secretary of State and created the European Recovery program which became known as the Marshall Plan.

> The strongest people do not
> need constant praise to excel.

Examples of how arrogance and selfishness limit accomplishment surround us. They are more obvious than examples of humility because humble people *deliberately* avoid showcasing themselves.

Will Rogers' father was a wealthy Oklahoma businessman who owned 50,000 head of cattle, a bank, a livery stable and a racetrack. It would have been easy for young Will to follow his dad's desire for him to take over but he wanted to travel and make his own life. His line, "I never met a man I didn't like," captures the humility which made him the country's best known humorist, author, actor and columnist in the 1920's and 30's.

How to Test Your Selfishness Quotient (SQ)

If arrogance results mostly from undisciplined selfishness, how can we know if and when we are going too far? These questions will enable you to be more objective about your **SQ**.

Check one response for each item:

1. I get bored quickly.
   ☐Usually ☐Sometimes ☐Rarely
2. I prefer to talk than listen.
   ☐Usually ☐Sometimes ☐Rarely
3. Criticism is hard to accept.
   ☐Usually ☐Sometimes ☐Rarely
4. People believe I am impatient.
   ☐Usually ☐Sometimes ☐Rarely
5. People say I am unforgiving.
   ☐Usually ☐Sometimes ☐Rarely
6. I deserve more than I get.
   ☐Usually ☐Sometimes ☐Rarely
7. I prefer to work alone.
   ☐Usually ☐Sometimes ☐Rarely
8. I interrupt frequently.
   ☐Usually ☐Sometimes ☐Rarely
9. People say I don't show appreciation.
   ☐Usually ☐Sometimes ☐Rarely
10. People say I don't share credit.
    ☐Usually ☐Sometimes ☐Rarely

Key:

Score 5 points for each ***usually***
Score 3 points for each ***sometimes***
Score 1 point for each ***rarely***

10—20 points = **Low SQ**—You are perceived as a caring helper
20—35 points = **Mid SQ**—Trust is likely to be withheld
35—50 points = **High SQ**—Selfishness will encourage
suspicion, opposition and isolation.

Arrogance is vulnerable because:

- **It encourages us to believe we have little left to learn.**
- **It puts too much confidence in short-term success.**
- **It assumes that all hardship can be avoided**
- **It makes us susceptible to "yes men."**
- **It tends to shift blame to lower ranking people.**
- **It diminishes respect and blocks out trust—including customers.**

Let's examine each of these reasons more closely.

- **It encourages us to believe we have little left to learn.**

> Stop trying and you stop learning. Stop learning and you start dying.

Anthony J. Drexel funded some of the businesses that helped America become a world-class economic force in the late 1800's. They included Thomas Edison's Electric Co. and the banking syndicate that funded the Panama Canal. He also helped support construction of the railroads whose tracks linked the United States, and made national commerce possible.

Even as a youth, Anthony would rather be behind the scenes than in the spotlight. Throughout his life, he was in the background as a mentor to U.S. bankers, publishers and presidents, and so left his mark.

He realized that a strong banker could help stabilize volatile financial markets. He did just that when the federal government could not pay salaries and fund the Civil War. In 1863, near the end of the war, Drexel met Gen. Ulysses S. Grant, who six years later became president and often turned to him for economic advice.

> ### Evaluate potential from the neck up.

- **It puts too much confidence in short-term success.**

Jim Boeheim was coach of the Syracuse University basketball team for 27 years before his team won the NCAA tournament championship in 2003. But he doesn't believe he became a good coach just because he finally reached that pinnacle.

"That's absolute foolishness," he says. He believes in being consistent, and that the only way to accurately judge coaches is on how their teams perform over the long haul.

He began his career at Syracuse as a player 41 years ago and quickly earned a starting berth next to perhaps the greatest player in Syracuse history, Dave Bing. Getting that slot was because of Boeheim's persistence on the court, along with his humility. His drive was admired, while his low-key approach impressed other players. He "was very unassuming," Bing said. "He loved the game and he knew what his skill level was and what he could do."

Wanting to get into coaching somehow, he started by taking a position at his alma mater as a golf coach. In 1972, he was named a full-time assistant basketball coach. By 1976, when the head coach retired, Jim Boeheim, then only 32, got the job he always wanted. The Carrier Dome, which seats over 33,000 for basketball, has led the nation in attendance every season since it opened. The team won 100 games in his first four years (no other coach had done that)—and 350 games faster than any other team in history. His consistency over time is what counts most to him.

- **It assumes that all hardship can be avoided**

As a young girl, Juliette Gordon Low came down with brain fever and lost most of her hearing. At 25, her doctor tried injecting silver nitrate in her ear, but it didn't help and by her mid-20s, she was practically deaf. When she married William Mackay Low in 1886, a grain of thrown rice lodged in her ear, causing an infection that further deteriorated her hearing.

Most others might have withdrawn, but not Juliette. She was always positive. Her attitude enabled her to found the world's largest voluntary organization for girls, with over 3.5 million members—the Girl Scouts of America, originally named the American Girl Guide troop. In weekly meetings, Low taught the young girls independence via careers, and service to society. For the girls to learn leadership, Low encouraged them to lead their own groups. Adult guides were not considered leaders, but advisors. To encourage the group to be self-supporting, the girls made their own uniforms, and raised money with bake sales, the precursors of the Girl Scout Cookies.

- **It makes us susceptible to "yes men."**

When people realize they will be punished for disagreeing or asking tough questions, they will play it safe and let you make the mistakes. The best leaders encourage challenge to get the best answers.

Bill Sharman's name may not be a household word. But he's the only man in the history of the National Basketball Association to win championships as a player, coach, general manager and team president. Throughout his long career, he's been part of a record 15 championship teams. With a great work ethic, always dedicated, he has relied heavily on communication skills. "To be a good coach, you have to get the respect of the players. You've got to get to know each one individually," he believes. Former Laker player and now assistant coach, Jim Cleamons says, "Coach Sharman is a very humble person. I think that helps him in his dealings with other people."

Sharman stressed a team-oriented concept, as opposed to relying on a couple of great players. He never managed by using intimidation or fear tactics and made players feel like part of the decision-making process. Those methods helped the 1971-72 Lakers become one of the greatest teams in the history of the NBA.

> Humble people prefer
> to be an example than
> to give advice.

- **It tends to shift blame to lower ranking people.**

David Pottruck often disagreed with his boss when he was president of the Charles Schwab Corporation Operating Company. Their arguments almost forced Pottruck to leave the company until he decided that the problem was his to solve. He told his boss that he would never disagree with him in public again. It worked. He was able to express his ideas without confrontation and everyone benefited.

General Peter Pace has a lot of clout in the Marine Corps. But he is always urging his subordinates to challenge him. He has a rule that he will not end a meeting without asking his subordinates for their recommendations. Pace wants full disclosure. He wants people to express truth as they see it even when more powerful people are involved.

General Pace's outlook underscores my personal conviction that the worst act of disloyalty is to allow your boss to make a preventable mistake.

- **It diminishes respect and blocks out trust—including customers.**

> Trust is inseparable
> from truth.

Marshall Field's dedication helped him establish what became the world's most profitable retail store. As a youth, he began working as a stockboy and noted the store's inventory, tracking what sold well and what didn't. Field was an innovator, who stayed focused on owning his own business one day. Partnered with Levi Zeigler Leiter, he opened a department store on State Street in Chicago in 1868. By 1881, Field bought out his partner and renamed the store Marshall Field. He took risks and extended customers liberal credit. Truly believing "the customer is always right," he allowed returns with a smile. Trying to outguess customers' needs, he thought they'd leave if they got hungry, so he devised the first department store restaurant. Window displays and advertising were Field's specialties. Among the first to display prices prominently, he instituted the no-haggling, one-price policy.

Field was known to extend his consideration not just to the customer, but also to his employees. One icy cold morning, he inquired, "How many boys came down without overcoats and mittens?" and then ordered, "Outfit them all, and say nothing about it." He felt that a comfortable worker would be a better worker. Towards the end of his life, he was a generous philanthropist, establishing the Field Museum of Natural History and giving to the University of Chicago. Despite his wealth, Field tried to remember where he came from, and live frugally, often walking to work.

> Integrity
> is measured only in action,
> never intent.

General Joe Stilwell was multi-lingual. In the army for 42 years, he learned Spanish, French and Mandarin Chinese. What was important to him? Not glory, rank, nor praise. Getting the job done—now that meant something to him! Nicknamed "Vinegar Joe," Stilwell was a soldier's soldier. Once, as the Japanese army threatened their positions, he refused a flight out, and instead led 114 people on a 150-mile retreat to safety.

Once while leading a prisoner along a jungle trail, he found a dehydrated comrade, who had collapsed alongside the path. Although he himself was dehydrated, he marched the prisoner and carried the soldier back to his unit. He neither received nor sought any praise.

Stilwell often sat with enlisted men in casual dress, and discussed tactical problems. They referred to him as "Uncle Joe." At the rank of brigadier general, he was offered an aide, but refused. He thought it was pretentious. He liked to say, "The higher a monkey climbs a pole, the more you see of his behind." Stilwell's peers rated him our country's best corps commander.

Positive people do not
follow negative people.

2

Loyalty Works Both Ways

Although not unique to humans, loyalty goes beyond the innate instincts in our genes into the arenas of choice, preference and stability.

Without it, individuals do not stay together. It is the glue which bonds groups. Once achieved it is hard to break. Once broken, it is difficult to mend and leaves indelible scars. A common temptation is to expect loyalty before it is earned. Attempts to "demand" it fail because they are interpreted as one sided. Only when loyalty is given can it be expected to be returned.

Why do humble people attract a loyal response?

- **They do not openly resist others' self-centered behavior.**
- **They allow others to try to get what they want without overt resistance.**
- **They question conduct they can't condone but do not criticize caustically.**
- **They don't complain about their help.**
- **They lead by example not words.**

- **They help people see the advantages of unselfish behavior.**
- **They volunteer.**
- **They appreciate others' talents.**
- **They are thankful.**

Here are the reasons I have observed:

- **They do not openly resist others' self-centered behavior.**

Althea Gibson never gave up on tennis. Born in Silver, S.C., in 1927, when prejudice made it hard for a black tennis player to compete, she nonetheless won 11 Grand Slam titles. Gibson broke down barriers in becoming the first black player to win both Wimbledon and the U.S. Open. Inducted into the International Tennis Hall of Fame in 1971, she still deserves credit today for opening doors for minorities.

Provided with financial and coaching support from two doctors, she moved into the home of Dr. and Mrs. Hubert Eaton in North Carolina at age 19 to practice tennis and finish high school. Before and after school and on weekends, Gibson worked with Eaton on drills to continue to improve her game. Summers were spent in Virginia, taking lessons from Dr. Robert Johnson. There she had access to an automated ball machine, which helped her develop her strokes. As her skills increased, she had trouble controlling her temper when losing. It wasn't until she realized this weakness that she began to win consistently.

She could see that certain types of behavior and etiquette were expected on the court, and she had to work at not expressing her frustrations. She also continued to battle the one obstacle, which she could not change, that stood in her way: the color of her skin.

After graduating from Florida A&M in 1953, she started coaching men's tennis at Lincoln University in Missouri, which helped her stay at the top of her game. She became the first black person to win the French Open in 1956. The next year, Gibson won the U.S. Open at Forest Hills. At the not so tender age of 30, she won Wimbledon, and then defended both titles again in 1958. Named Female Athlete of the Year in both years, Althea Gibson broke new ground.

- **They allow others to try to get what they want without overt resistance.**

Their influence is felt as listeners rather than "change enforcers." The speaker of the U.S. House of Representatives, Dennis Hastert, is convinced that his most important job is to be an effective listener. Only then can he help people salvage some of what they want even in extremely controversial political situations. Most experts agree that his reputation for being fair but firm won him the job as Speaker and continues to earn praise.

To receive loyalty
think "we."

- **They question conduct they can't condone but do not criticize caustically.**

Marvin Gralnick, CEO of Chico's FAS women's specialty store was all set for retirement. In fact, he enjoyed every minute of it, while it lasted. But once he's pledged his loyalty to something, he's not about to give that up. As soon as he realized the company was in trouble, he and his wife came out of retirement to offer help.

He tries not to let his ego interfere. He feels that is a big mistake made by many in business. No one person is more important than the rest. Not even the CEO, he says. By surrounding himself with team players, there is no need for superstars. He chooses talented, flexible, extroverts who are emotionally stable. His show of respect for others instills a team spirit, which he believes is Chico's secret to success.

And with earnings growing at an average annual rate of 78% since 1996, and sales by an average of 27% annually, he gives all credit to the team. Gralnick follows his gut feeling and says, " . . . it's not just intuition. There's a lot of strength and knowledge that people block out because they don't trust themselves."

> The quickest route to
> gain loyalty is empathy—
> protecting others' dignity.

- **They don't complain about their help.**

Eileen Filicicchia is determined to do all she can to keep her husband alive. Frank has a 20-year history of very serious heart problems. Most days she feels like stress is running their lives, and the rate keeps going up. It all started in November of 1980, when he had a massive heart attack.

Throughout the '80s, he had several angiograms and bypass surgery. He seemed to be doing well until July of '99, when he passed out on the kitchen floor. Eileen called 911 and will never forget the doctor who told her, "Don't worry, I won't let him die." Two more surgeries followed: one to insert an Implantable Cardioverter Defibrillator (ICD) unit, and another to remove a pacemaker.

She drives him everywhere and pushes his wheelchair at the hospital where he waits while she completes her rehab sessions following her own heart surgery. Eileen says simply, "We're not giving up, and we're not complaining either."

- **They lead by example not words.**

Rarely eloquent speakers, humble people let the results of their actions putting others ahead of them convey their message. For example, who is the winner in this story?

And the winner is . . . ?

. . . A few years ago, at the Seattle Special Olympics, nine contestants, all physically or mentally disabled, assembled at the starting line for the 100-yard dash.

At the gun, they all started out, not exactly in a dash, but with a relish to run the race to the finish and win. All that is, except one little boy who stumbled on the asphalt, tumbled over a couple of times, and began to cry.

The other eight heard the boy cry. They slowed down and looked back. Then they all turned around and went back . . . every one of them.

One girl with Down Syndrome bent down and kissed him and said, "This will make it better." Then all nine linked arms and walked together to the finish line. Everyone in the stadium stood, and the cheering went on for several minutes. People who were there are still telling the story.

Why? Because deep down we know this: What matters in this life is more than winning for ourselves. What matters in this life is helping others win, even if it means slowing down and changing our course.

> A candle loses nothing by lighting another candle.

- **They help people see the advantages of unselfish behavior.**

At age 11, David Levitt learned about Kentucky Harvest, a not-for-profit organization that gets surplus food to people who need it. He read that 27% of our nation's food was wasted, while some people were hungry.

David asked if his school could join a local program to use leftovers from the cafeteria. Discovering that district health regulations prevented them from participating, he began to cut the red tape by appealing directly to the school board. But then there were state regulations requiring specific containers, which the school could not afford. Undaunted, he appealed to the corporation that made the bags. He got the help he needed.

A year later, the program, involving 94 schools, had sent over 350,000 pounds of cafeteria surplus to local food banks and homeless shelters.

- **They volunteer.**

The highest honor in law enforcement is the Police Officer of the Year Award, sponsored by the International Chiefs of Police. In 2001 it was given to Joseph Farina for his brave rescue of 20 people from a fire in Newark, NJ. Farina, however, contrasts his action with the people of 9/11, who he feels are real heroes. His humility is no surprise to his colleagues. They see him consistently helping co-workers. "The smallest problems are important to him," a fellow officer says. "He takes that one extra step." He has risked his life more than once to rescue people from fires, without protective gear.

Farina had a good job at a paper company. He left and took a pay cut to become a policeman. Why? Because he wanted to help others more than anything else. When his younger brother Emile became involved with drugs and alcohol, he helped him back on the right track. Joseph said that part of the bail loan he gave him had to be used for rehab. Emile, now successful, says his brother saved his life.

- **They appreciate others' talents.**

Nick Irons certainly wasn't chasing fame or fortune when he swam the entire length of the Mississippi River or bicycled 10,000 miles across the U.S. He was following a dream of finding a way to eradicate Multiple Sclerosis (MS), a chronic degenerative central nervous system disease that affects approximately 1.5 million people in the world.

His father, John Irons, a physician, has suffered from MS for over 20 years. Ever since Nick found out about his dad's illness at the age of 12, he believed that research could find a cure, and wondered what he could do about it.

He hit upon the idea of swimming the mighty Mississippi—over 1500 miles—along the way, he'd gather pledges and donations to fight MS. He dove into the river on June 1, 1997, and four months later, finished in Baton Rouge, LA. He made it, and fulfilled his goal.

But he didn't stop there. Once again, in 2000, he began a 10,000 mile bike ride across and around America, gathering donations and pledges. In less than 5 months, he completed that goal also. Back in 1995, when Nick first conceived the idea to swim the Mississippi, he mentioned it to his parents. Instead of being shocked, and questioning his logic, they simply asked how they could help. That's what it's all about. Nick knew he couldn't do it alone, so he found people who were willing to help.

> Hardship exposes three things—problems, winners and losers.

- **They are thankful.**

Angelo Giuseppe Roncalli (1881-1963) is better known as Pope John XXIII. He was the third of 13 children in his immediate family, but there were 28 mouths to feed in his extended family, which included parents, grandparents, uncles, aunts and children. "We were very poor, but so was everyone, so we didn't realize that we lacked anything," he said.

Writer Norman Cousins had an audience with Pope John XXIII in 1962, and instantly realized something he hadn't expected to see—humility. Known for his humble, self-effacing ways, he convened Vatican Council II in 1962 to try to heal wounds and bring together Christians of all denominations from around the World.

Growing up in poverty made him more generous. He felt that was what he learned, by being part of a loving family.

3

The Upside of Defeat

Adversity does not
develop values.
It exposes them.

Humble people worry less about defeat because they are not as impressed by the prizes of victory. They are happy when you are happy—and they are even happier if they have helped you in the process. They are not immune from feelings of rejection, loss and defeat but they are not permanently affected by them.

We learn from our successes but we live by how we adjust to defeat. That's because recovering from defeat usually requires more of us than maintaining success. Staying on a success path can become a habit but bouncing back from defeat requires new skills and disciplines each time.

How do humble people cope with defeat?

- **They view setbacks as a stimulus to keep climbing.**
- **They act on their convictions.**

- **They overcome handicaps.**
- **They don't seek perfect conditions.**
- **They transfer credit to those they help.**
- **They avoid harsh judgment.**
- **They try new ways to be helpful.**
- **They build bridges.**
- **They are not easily discouraged.**
- **They show gratitude.**

Humble people consider their ability to be persistent as a positive influence:

- **They view setbacks as a stimulus to keep climbing.**

> Difficulty may not only slow you down, it may show you up.

Dale Carnegie is a name known to most people. With over 50 million people buying his books in 30 languages, and his training courses still thriving today, it's no wonder. But the father of the modern self-help movement found little success in his own life, neither personally, nor professionally until 1936, when he published the now famous, *How to Win Friends and Influence People*. A college dropout, he tried numerous careers including farming, sales, writing, and acting. None succeeded. He practically lost his shirt in the 1929 stock market crash. His first marriage ended in calamitous divorce.

Success never came easy to him. Not even in the self-help arena. It was hard because he was shy by nature. He felt self-confidence was the key to success in all pursuits, yet never totally conquered his own fear of public speaking. One way he tried was by lecturing livestock on his father's farm for hours on different subjects. The only way, he believed, to develop self-confidence was to persist in doing the things you fear until you have a number of successes to look back upon.

He claimed the reason he wrote *How to Win Friends and Influence People* was because he blundered so frequently himself.

John North Willys' formal education stopped at age 18, when his father passed away. But he was bright, and didn't let that stop him. At only 20, he and a friend opened a laundry. They sold it just four years later for a few hundred dollars and put that money into another business, a bicycle shop.

He kept taking what he earned, and reinvesting it in new businesses. Where some saw only clouds, he saw the silver lining. He followed his passion, which led him to the emerging automobile business. Taking the Overland Company back from receivership, he renamed it the Willys-Overland Company. By 1912, Overland averaged sales of 26,000 cars per year, topped only by the Ford Motor Company.

Willys endeared himself to his employees by doing things like taking them all out to play baseball at a nearby playing field.

Then, during a recession, Willys hired Walter Percy Chrysler to take a spot as Executive Vice President, at a reported million-dollar salary—a tidy sum in those days. Immediately, Chrysler cut Willys' salary from $150,000 to $75,000. Willys took this as strictly business, nothing personal, and reportedly laughed. Rather than form resentment, the two men actually forged a close friendship, and Willys used his experience to set the company back on its financial feet again. Eventually the company produced the best known vehicle in World War II—the Jeep.

- **They act on their convictions.**

> I may be impressed
> with your convictions but
> am convinced only by what
> you do.

These days, Jamie Saunders doesn't take a thing for granted. The high school senior class president found out she had cancer when she was a freshman. While Jamie was beginning to fight for her own life, she realized she also wanted to make a difference for others.

Her visit to the impoverished Caribbean island nation of Haiti for nearly three weeks in the summer of '02 hit home for her. She could see the contrast with living in a relatively safe, secure and wealthy country like she did.

Saunders has also had similar experiences much closer to home. She's helped re-tile floors, re-tar roofs, paint homes and work in a soup kitchen in nearby neighborhoods. She also volunteered by repairing and painting homes in the next town as part of a "Christmas in April" project.

Two years ago, she went to Appalachia where she helped with service projects. Jamie says she didn't realize the positive effect she could have on others until faced with her own illness.

- **They overcome handicaps.**

> The difference between
> strength and weakness
> is will power.

At only 5 foot 8 and 137 pounds, Ben Hogan knew he'd have to fight to distinguish himself from his peers. Since consistency is so important in golf, he was the first to hit thousands of balls each week, to learn exactly how his own swing worked. From that he determined what was needed while playing under stress.

The first seven years of Hogan's pro career were winless. Often in the early 1930's, he couldn't afford to get to the next tournament. But he didn't give up.

When Ben was just 9 years old, he witnessed his dad's suicide. What may have destroyed someone else, made Ben even stronger.

He never took a day off. Practice, persistence and perseverance were the keys to his success. Hogan won 9 major championships. He is third in all-time career wins behind only Sam Snead and Jack Nicklaus. At age 37, Hogan had a near-fatal head on crash—his car hit a Greyhound bus outside of El Paso, TX. That next year, he managed to win his second U.S. Open anyway. Then just three years later, he won the Masters, U.S. Open and the British Open. That year, he was the recipient of a tickertape parade in Manhattan.

- **They don't seek perfect conditions.**

> ## Perfection is an illusion.

Seattle Sutton believes she must prove every day that you can build a successful company based on treating your customers and employees fairly, and delivering on promises. A registered nurse who worked with her husband's medical practice, she found many patients who said they would follow a healthier diet if someone else would do the work. Sutton knew what they were saying was true, so she made up her mind to be the one to do it.

The small handful of customers she began with has blossomed to over 120,000 per week funneling through 100 distributors. The company launched with a $1,000 investment now employs around 150 people and grosses $13 million in annual sales.

> ## When you work with good people, learn what to do.
> —
> ## When you work with bad people, learn what not to do.

Dodgers' Catcher Roy Campanella was a big star, three-time MVP, who never acted the part. Success brought him fame, but it didn't change him a bit. One night, at a dinner, Sandy Koufax tried to give Roy all the credit for calling a good game Koufax had pitched, but he wouldn't take it. "Son, the ball was in your hands," he said.

Campanella believed it was important to mix with the pitchers off the field, understand their personalities, personal lives, hopes, dreams, and ambitions. He felt a pitcher could tell when his catcher was not confident. He helped pitchers Koufax and Don Drysdale make it into the Hall of Fame. Campanella himself was only the second black player elected into Baseball's Hall of Fame in 1969.

Roy fought for the rights of minorities, and in 1958, when disabled in a car crash, he took up the cause of people with disabilities. As a quadriplegic after the accident, his doctor told him that he could only help 10%, but the other 90% must be Roy's own effort. Once he began reading the Bible his mother gave him, he knew he was on his way back, and was going to make it. Expected to survive 10-15 years, his positive outlook enabled him to have 35 more years to show what he meant by the title of his book, "It's Good to Be Alive."

- **They transfer credit to those they help.**

William Wilson, better known as Bill W. has been a friend and lifesaver to millions. He once was unable to help even himself out of the throes of alcoholism. He realized though, that mere willpower was not the answer. Soul-searching, however, did hold the key, and turning to another alcoholic struggling to overcome addiction helped. He founded Alcoholics Anonymous so he could reach out and help others.

As a child, Wilson was nearly always ill, battling the stigma of coming from a broken home and the death of his high school sweetheart. He didn't succumb to depression, but instead joined the military and pursued higher education. He was successful on Wall Street, until his drinking made him unemployable. By 1933, he and his wife could not survive, but for the charity of others.

In 1935, Alcoholics Anonymous was founded by Wilson and an old drinking buddy, Dr. Robert Smith. Smith's family implored him to allow Wilson 15 minutes to talk with him. The conversation lasted several hours, and Bill thought that if he could stay sober by talking with someone else, then others could benefit also.

Because anonymity is an important aspect of AA's work, last names are never used in groups, and Bill W. refused public honor, not accepting a degree from Yale or an appearance on the cover of Time magazine. Nor did he accept money for speaking engagements or counseling. The difference this humble man has made in the lives of millions is immeasurable.

- **They avoid harsh judgment.**

Humble people have learned how to avoid harsh judgments about themselves or others, which diminish potential for future accomplishments. They realize that loss of confidence crushes initiative, that condemnation kills a willingness to take risks and that extreme punishment causes most people to hide from any action which might increase their vulnerability. To attract people who will venture forward without prodding requires selecting those who want to be responsible.

William Upjohn was such a man. After years of failure and criticism, he developed a coating for pills which held the ingredients together but was easily crushed and digested by stomach acid. By staying positive about his company, even in hard times, he was able to get bank loans and pioneered employee benefits including group insurance, a cafeteria and shorter work week. Upjohn's motto served him well, "The more fears you entertain, the less initiative you will have." Although he died in 1932, his legacy lives on in Kalamazoo, Michigan, his home town. In 2000 he was named, "Person of the Century."

> To forget and move on is wise.
> To blame and resent is stupid.

- **They try new ways to be helpful.**

Sister Elizabeth Kenny first examined an infant with polio in 1911. She had no idea what to do, and sent a telegram to the physician she worked for asking him to help. He knew of no treatment, and advised her to do her best. She wasted no time. Sr. Kenny had seen muscles in spasm before, and knew heat could relax them, so she covered the infant's legs with heated blankets. She also exercised the paralyzed muscles.

Amazingly, the little girl recovered within days. In fact, all six children in her district who had polio recovered with Kenny's aid. Her methods were opposed by the medical community, but she kept going. Her intervention soon helped thousands of children, and her principles were used in the formation of the physical therapy profession.

Born in New South Wales, Australia in 1880, she worked on her parents' farm. After breaking her wrist falling off her horse, she questioned the doctor about how muscles work. She wanted to know more, so she devised her own version of a skeleton with pulleys.

At age 16, Kenny graduated from college and began a nursing career with on-the-job training. She worked her way up to head nurse or "sister" in the Australian Army. By the early 1930's, polio had become a worldwide epidemic. Word of her success traveled round the world, and brought patients from many countries.

At the time, most doctors considered her work "quackery," but that didn't stop her. In 1940, she moved to the U.S. hoping to find a more receptive audience for her treatment. In spite of obstacles, she kept at it, healed hundreds more children and finally gained acceptance for her ideas. In 1952, she was voted the "most admirable woman" in America.

Sr. Kenny didn't work for fame or fortune. She never accepted pay for services. What mattered to her was the happiness and health of the children she saved. That number reached 10,000 by the time she died in 1952. Three years later the Salk polio vaccine was discovered.

- **They build bridges.**

Thomas Watson, Sr. wanted to put employees first. His integrity was impeccable. He did not believe in separating character issues from business or personal life. Once, when a regional sales manager had a car accident that killed his infant son, Watson made sure there was someone at the hospital to help through the crisis, and made sure all the hospital bills were paid.

Watson was at the helm in the rise of the international behemoth, which became IBM. He could see that the late 20th century would be the "information age." He also understood the significance of corporate culture and focused on it as a strategic asset. Even during the Great Depression, he refused to lay people off but instead increased the Research &Development budget.

IBM not only survived, but thrived after the 1935 passage of the Social Security Act, with its demand for better payroll tracking. With other companies cutting back staff, IBM provided the machines needed to replace them. By the time Watson retired, the company had a manufacturing presence in over 80 countries around the world.

- **They are not easily discouraged.**

> Failure is a prelude
> to winning.

Samuel Adams was the strongest voice of revolution in the early 1760's. The British considered him extremely dangerous, while the Americans called him the "Father of American Independence."

His incendiary editorials to Boston newspapers led readers to believe that city was on the verge of revolution. He also wrote articles under almost a dozen pseudonyms, calling for independence.

Adams taught many other patriots his methods, including Paul Revere, John Hancock and John Adams, who relied on him for guidance. He kept a close eye on them and won them over to his position against the British.

Adams realized that the ultimate goal was more important than his own personal gain. His behind-the-scenes speechwriting for Hancock and others was never credited to him. A major organizer of the Boston Tea Party, he didn't admit to leading it, because he preferred people perceive it as a spontaneous uprising.

To prove his point, Adams avoided the pompous formalities and traditions of the monarchy he wanted Americans to overthrow. His greatest satisfaction was that his years of opposition finally resulted in the beginning of a full-scale war of independence.

Writer William Lloyd Garrison had no wealth, power or formal education, but was determined to end slavery. His mouthpiece was the weekly newspaper, the Liberator, which he founded in 1831.

Garrison did not believe in conceding rights to slave-owners, or postponing the end of slavery. He supported his arguments with both the New Testament and the Declaration of Independence. His reasons for opposing slavery were based on ethics, which helped build an anti-slavery mentality.

President Lincoln credited Garrison with swaying Northern opinion toward the abolition of slavery, without delay. Lincoln issued the Emancipation Proclamation while the Civil War was still going on, partly due to his influence.

Garrison was not afraid to risk his life for the cause he believed in. Frequently threatened with physical harm from both Southerners and Northerners, he stood strong, and was never intimidated.

Steven Levitt, 36, is a very unusual economist. He deliberately uses his knowledge of economics in fields where it is rarely applied like street gangs, crime, abortion, corruption and cheating in schools.

He has found, for example, strong evidence that abortion is directly related to crime because crime dropped sharply 18 years after 1973 when abortion became legal. Further, he discovered that the 5 states that had legalized abortion earlier were the first to experience crime declines.

Levitt's reputation is built on persistence. He realizes that most of his ideas may not work so moves on quickly to the next. The key he says is to "learn how to fail quickly because every hour spent on a failing project could be spent on a successful one." He doesn't try to manufacture evidence—he moves on.

- **They show gratitude.**

Why is expressing appreciation so difficult for so many people? What holds us back? Why can't "thank you" be easy to say? The answer probably involves the reluctance to admit we couldn't or didn't do something for ourselves. Somehow "strong" personalities think they diminish themselves when they openly show gratitude.

But humble people know better. They realize that it is a sign of *their* strength to be thankful for favors. They understand that appreciation, like flattery, motivates the receiver to be more cooperative in the future, to be a better team player and to look for more opportunities to contribute.

When we know that something we have said or done is appreciated, two things happen: 1) our respect for that person increases and 2) we are likely to find more ways to be helpful. Both are essential building blocks for the success of any group in any endeavor.

4

When Pride Goes Too Far

> Pride says—
> this is the way it is!
> Integrity says—
> let's discuss.
> Humility asks—
> what do you think?

Pride—a feeling of satisfaction about accomplishment—is a good thing. But it can go too far and backfire. Then, two things happen—the personal satisfaction is lost and we alienate the people we were trying to influence or impress.

Pride is a two edged sword. One edge enables us to be competitive. The other can be a handicap when it becomes vanity and encourages people to resist, avoid or ignore us.

The first question is, "Who follows 'Me First' people?" Isn't it usually those who don't realize when pride is excessive?

For example:

When we think of pride and fierce competitiveness, we often think of Olympic Athletes. Emil Zatopek, who died at age 78, was still the only person who won the 3 longest track events in one Olympics. He set records in all 3, and it was his first marathon race ever.

Called the "Human Locomotive" for his powerful running abilities, "Human" was the key word. He was an ardent defender of human rights, dignity and freedom. Standing up to the Soviet invasion of Czechoslovakia in 1968 meant a demotion to a menial job, but he would not be silenced.

His track record spoke for itself. He set 18 world records, and four of them won him Olympic gold. His compassion was evident when he gave one of his gold medals to Australian Ron Clarke. Clarke had also set 18 world records, but only won one bronze medal in two Olympics.

When Zatopek ran, he always had a pained expression on his face. He said that came from "not being talented enough to run and smile at the same time."

Character Counts

Former law professor and businessman, Michael Josephson had an awakening when his first son was born. He taught ethics at prestigious law schools, but he felt the ethics code was sorely lacking. He also had a very profitable business, which he sold in 1985 for over $10 million. Knowing that he didn't have to earn another cent for the rest of his life freed him to spend $1 million to open an ethics institute and serve as its president without pay.

Best known for the *Character Counts Coalition*, his institute advocates *Six Pillars of Character*—trustworthiness, respect, responsibility, fairness, caring and citizenship. The coalition includes more than 350 youth and educational organizations, who agree to teach their youth the Six Pillars. The same principles apply to profit and non-profit organizations alike. Josephson says competency without character will defeat itself and vice-versa.

Josephson also believes that the self-respect entailed in goodness outweighs any gains motivated by greed. He contends that good ethics promote better business and better relationships, when people realize that eventually bad behavior will ruin them.

William Wrigley Jr. had—or caused—more than his share of trouble in school. He was finally expelled at age 13. But he had already developed a strong work ethic. He left home at age 11, to become a newsboy on the streets of New York City. Later, working for his father's soap company, he was a natural salesman. A favorite technique was knowing a potential customer's patterns. Wrigley got up early to meet one prospect every day for a month, until he finally purchased some soap.

Another time, a salesman tried to sell Wrigley a promotional item. The deal they negotiated was so tight, the salesman claimed he'd be losing money on it. So Wrigley tore the contract in half, saying he didn't want anyone losing money on a deal with him. Wrigley understood that in the long run, a company should not succeed at the expense of the people it does business with.

Although most people know that Wrigley sold chewing gum, few realize that it is one of the top companies in the U.S in terms of profitability. In 1919 he bought a controlling interest in the Chicago Cubs. In that same year, he purchased Catalina Island, off California's coast and developed it into one of this country's premier resorts. Wrigley's creed: "A man's doubts and fears are his worst enemies."

Professor Stephen Ambrose did not consider himself an academician. He believed he was a writer and his more than 30 history books prove it. Yet in Ambrose's mind there was no "secret" to it. It was done by working long hours each day, practically seven days a week. He enjoyed the diligent research, reading the available information and choosing the most representative illustrations of common themes or actions.

He was very down to earth and loved talking to people. Never comfortable in suits or ties, he liked eating in diners, and staying at inexpensive hotels. When writing about

World War II, he visited all the battlefields in Europe several times. He was accompanied by veterans, some officers up to the rank of general, others drafted or enlisted personnel, many privates. They shared their first-hand memories of their D-Day experiences.

He witnessed Douglas Brinkley, his successor at the National D-Day Museum, being lambasted by a commentator who criticized a paper he presented. Ambrose walked right up to the two of them and loudly praised Brinkley. He advised him not to listen to the criticism and told him he'd be a great historian one day. Stephen Ambrose wrote books not for entertainment, but for education. He passed along those intangible qualities of wisdom, judgment, enthusiasm and his intense love of America.

> Those who deliberately
> make things more complex
> are intellectual fools.

What egotists must learn:

- **Accept Criticism**
- **Do the Right Thing**
- **Stoop Down to Teach**
- **Overcome Adversity**

To control their impulses to dominate and keep pride from becoming a handicap, egotists must learn to:

- **Accept Criticism**

Captain John Wesley Powell survived the Civil War, but had to have his right arm amputated above the elbow, after being wounded during the Battle of Shiloh. That did not stop him from returning to combat and earning a promotion to major. After the war, he dreamed of riding the Colorado River through the Grand Canyon. He wanted to be the first to navigate the entire length of the river, and although it seemed unlikely, he turned his dream into reality.

A 35-year-old unproven quantity, he barely knew the wide-open west, and had to finance his own expedition from practically empty pockets. He faced seemingly insurmountable obstacles, losing rations, boats sinking, even losing crew members. Somehow, he remained optimistic. He often scaled the cliffs himself, with only one arm, to examine the surrounding areas.

When they reached the spot where the Colorado and Green rivers met, they were able to complete one of the only remaining gaps in the U.S. map. By August of 1869, they were faced with daunting circumstances again—towering walls on both sides of them, few rations, and using driftwood for oars. But the majesty and beauty of their surroundings were not lost on Powell. When they were faced with the worst conditions yet, Powell wanted to continue by water, whereas three of his crew members did not. They left to try and continue by land, but it seems they never made it out. Their remains were not found.

The expedition lasted almost 100 days. They rowed down 1,000 miles of river and went down over a mile in elevation. Those that survived lived through whirlpools, poisonous snakes, and rock slides. Although Powell was hailed as a national hero, he remained always humble and eager to share his discoveries with others. He was named Director of the U.S. Geological Survey in 1881.

- **Do the Right Thing**

> To avoid the unknown is
> to walk away from life.

Long before he became Chief Justice of the Supreme Court, Earl Warren wanted to "do the right thing." He learned integrity and a good work ethic from his parents' example. In fact, in many of his positions, he often worked till midnight.

After almost 15 years as a prosecutor, 10 as governor of California, and several as Attorney General, Warren was well prepared when chosen in 1953 to become chief justice.

He valued good relationships with people, so he introduced himself to literally everyone who worked in the building—from elevator operators, to clerks and secretaries. Warren relied on the other justices for help, instead of using his own authority to make decisions. He visited people in chambers, finding ways to reach agreement. Adept at coalition building, he could reach unanimous decisions when they seemed hopelessly blocked. And many authorities believe that no justice since has mastered these skills as well.

> Few outcomes are certain.
> Keep trying.

Robin Yount was not the biggest celebrity in baseball. His greatest legacy is that he always put his team above himself. He did not beat Cal Ripkin's record for most consecutive games, but is the only player in major league history to have played over 1,000 games in the shortstop position, and another 1,000+ in the outfield. But most of all Yount was respected for his humility.

He would play, no matter how bad he felt. Whether he was injured or sick, if he was able to put on his uniform, he played.

He was named American League MVP in both '82 and '89, in two different positions, shortstop and center field. Yount was also named American League player of the decade for the 1980's. He made the all-star team three times, and was inducted into the Baseball Hall of Fame in 1999.

- **Stoop Down to Teach**

The essence of brilliance
is to simplify,
not complicate.

Anne Sullivan became a teacher almost as famous as her student, Helen Keller. She contracted an eye disease at age 5 and lost most of her vision. Her mother died when Anne was young, and her father, who had problems with alcohol, left the family shortly thereafter.

While in the state poorhouse, Sullivan met two women who helped her with her feelings of loss and abandonment. She truly enjoyed their company, as they read books to her. She wanted to learn more, and was finally able to attend a school for the blind.

At age 20 she took a job as a teacher for 6 year old Helen Keller, a girl who was deaf, blind and mute since the age of 18 months. When Sullivan arrived, Keller was behaving like a wild animal. Helen knew nothing of manners, grabbing food from others, throwing tantrums whenever opposed. Although her task seemed impossible, for the next 50 years,

Sullivan altruistically dedicated her life to tutoring Keller. Conquering her own obstacles helped her understand what Keller faced. Sullivan knew that she couldn't change anything but herself. She also felt strongly about what could be accomplished by people with disabilities.

Anne worked tirelessly, sometimes 24 hours a day trying to teach Helen to communicate. As Keller began to master reading, writing and even public speaking, Sullivan's reputation as a great teacher grew, and she never stopped lobbying for people with disabilities. When Sullivan celebrated her 67th birthday, Keller said, "Here's to my teacher, whose birthday was the Easter morning of my life."

- **Overcome Adversity**

Unless you have had at least one extended period in your life when you have felt lost and lonely, you will always be naïve. You will never be empathetic enough to understand a large percent of your relationships.

> Facing adversity
> is the only antidote
> for conceit.

Unfortunately we allow a sense of "one-upmanship" to put us in a never-ending race for status. There is only one cure—the desire to be helpful. Humility prevails when we drop status as a priority and replace it with a *compulsion* to be useful. Why? Because when we are needed, rank loses its impact. The highest ranking people can't do most things for themselves. That's why politicians hate to leave office. They realize how many privileges they will lose.

Discrimination based
on rank bars nobodies
of whatever stripe from
a fair chance at becoming
somebodies, and keeps
somebodies in their public
roles long after it's good for
them or anyone else.

—Robert W. Fuller, author,
Somebodies and Nobodies

Why can't we look beyond privileges and examine the
"rightness" of how people behave, the effect their actions
have on long-range consequences?

The 3 most challenging
questions in life are:

• what have I learned?
• what have I kept?
• what have I passed along?

5

How to Identify Pretenders

There is a difference between being happy (with joy) and satisfied (with circumstance); between contentment (with things as they are) and impatience (with slow progress).

> Today there is a circumstance
> but tomorrow there is only
> what I made of it.

Pretenders seem to always be unsettled. They fear discovery of their true motives and intentions. Authentically humble people abandon such fears because they prefer to not mask who they are and what they want.

Here is a question for you:

If you were 84 years old, wealthy and nationally known, would you get up at 3:30 a.m. 6 days a week to go to work? That's what Paul Harvey does, because he "hasn't found anything more interesting to do." Most people have heard of him, or heard from him, or both. He believes that news listeners or readers don't want to learn about some healthy, wealthy and happy man—that might make the reader feel bad about him or herself. The venerated radio newscaster recently told 2,000 senior citizens about enjoying life in spite of the gray hair and wrinkles. As proof he gave the conclusion reached by the New England Journal of Medicine that with nothing more than self-discipline, this generation can enjoy 100 years. Then, with a twinkle in his eye he added, "If life were logical, it would be men who ride side-saddle."

Successful people have fine-tuned their ability to differentiate between those whose motives are genuine and pretenders or hypocrites. They take the time needed to study revealing behaviors carefully and do not trust immediate impressions or what may be biased opinions.

> New nonsense
> is still nonsense.

Humble people are realists:

- **They learn to discount the exaggerations of status, wealth and power.**
- **They do not interpret winning any contest as sign of permanent superiority.**
- **They are sensitive to others' needs and preferences.**
- **They are genuinely interested in those who support them.**
- **They analyze why pretenders try to substitute charm and popularity for substance.**
- **They are sensitive to "infected" attitudes.**

It is not hard for humble people to spot pretenders because:

- **They learn to discount the exaggerations of status, wealth and power.**

> Reliable friends know little about your bank account.

At Baxter International, a $30.8 billion medical products company, CEO Harry J. Kraemer tries to balance work and home. He cares about people and proactively seeks out their views. His own home life is so important to him that he adopted his wife's surname (Jansen) as his middle name.

If he thinks he should leave an important meeting to coach his daughter's softball team, he does. He leads by example, so people know he's not just talking and encourages employees to do the same.

Kraemer's listening skills lead people to believe he is interested in everything they say. There's a genuine quality to it. Encouraging good communication with employees and customers has helped Baxter develop much-needed new products, including a small, convenient, portable kidney dialysis machine. He feels the key is keeping things simple, because they really are.

- **They do not interpret winning any contest as sign of permanent superiority.**

When football coach Eddie Robinson set a record as the first college coach to win 400 games, he said he wished he could split the credit and share it with all the players and assistants he had, because they all truly deserved it.

His humility is legendary. What made him more proud than all the victories was the graduation rate of his athletes.

While at Grambling (1941-98), 80% of his student-athletes graduated—45% was the national average.

Robinson's 57 years of coaching is topped only by his 60 years of marriage. His hard work and sincerity shows not only in his enduring marriage, but in all his relationships. He was inducted into the Horatio Alger Association of Distinguished Americans in 1988, and has been honored many times for his integrity.

When some people label him a great "black coach" he replies simply that he strives to be a "great American." And that he is.

Question: What sets Paul Newman apart as more than just a great actor? Answer: He's a *very* successful entrepreneur. In 1982, he founded Newman's Own, Inc. to produce his special blend of salad dressing. He donates all the profits to charity, but he didn't want that to appear on the label. He wasn't doing it for the accolades.

In 1985, he founded the Hole in the Wall Gang camp for children with cancer and serious blood diseases. From the beginning, it was funded by Newman's Own, to the tune of $10 million in start up costs. Newman's combination of passion, compassion, and humility is recognized by many others who help with his causes.

- **They are sensitive to others' needs and preferences.**

> Listen twice as much as you speak. We don't have 2 mouths and 1 ear.

Steve Case of America On-Line built an empire by listening to customers. He started young. Growing up in Honolulu, he had a paper route, like many kids his age. But he didn't restrict himself to delivering papers. He sold a wide variety of additional items to customers on his route.

From the age of 26 to 41, Case has been responsible for the tremendous growth of AOL, seeing subscribers grow to over 20 million, and his stock in AOL grow to over a billion dollars by the year 2000. He definitely realizes that arrogance is vulnerable, when he says, "You want people to be confident without being arrogant."

You might expect a man with his income to live on an estate, far removed from crowds and hassle. Instead, he lives in a modest home, regularly eats in the company lunchroom rather than a private dining room—and he tries to "not take myself too seriously."

> Those who value
> privileges above principles
> soon lose both.
>
> —Dwight D. Eisenhower

- **They are genuinely interested in those who support them.**

> You do not really know
> me unless you know a little
> about my successes and a lot
> about my failures.

John Lewis Kraft (1874-1953) was an amazing man, revered by employees and friends. He knew how to forge bonds of loyalty that last a lifetime. Until the number of Kraft employees surpassed 3,000, he knew each one by name. Many of them to this day have held on to the hand-crafted rings from American Jade, which he made and awarded employees for exemplary service.

In 1890, at age 16, he left home to help with the debt on the family's farm. First he sold eggs and within 2 years, had paid off the whole mortgage. But when new taxes drove him out of the egg business, he started making cheese. In 1903, with under $100 in capital—he rented a horse-drawn wagon. He and Paddy (his horse) began delivering cheese to local grocery stores.

Kraft wanted to learn more about cheese, in order to prolong its shelf life. By 1916, he patented processed cheese. For World War I, the army purchased massive quantities of canned cheese, which held up very well.

Even in the depths of the great Depression, Kraft was not a risk avoider. Instead, he launched an ad campaign for Miracle Whip, resulting in record advertising spending. That same year, he sponsored a radio show—the "Kraft Music Hall" to introduce new products. It quickly became a success. Kraft's products are still extremely popular,. and his respect for employees is the foundation of that heritage.

- **They analyze why pretenders try to substitute charm and popularity for substance.**

Thinking without acting
is harmless.
Acting without thinking
is dangerous.

- **They are sensitive to "infected" attitudes.**

> Integrity cannot be taught
> or trained. It becomes ingrained
> by following the example of
> honest, trustworthy people.

Terry Fox had something to prove—to himself and to the world. For over 20 weeks, he ran 26 miles a day (just under marathon distance), . . . a total of 3,339 miles. His purpose: to raise money for researching a cure for cancer.

But there's something else you should know—he did it on one leg. He had already lost his other leg to cancer. Only after 18 months of training was he able to run with the prosthetic leg.

Fox now believes that before the disease struck, he was a self-centered person. But after the illness, he felt compelled to help others. He wanted to demonstrate that anyone can make a difference so he single-handedly raised $1.7 million before having to return home for more treatment. The "Marathon of Hope" he started continues to this day. Now, over 50 countries hold Terry Fox runs each year to keep raising money for cancer research. Terry died in 1981, but his legacy lives on.

Quiet Dignity

How to Detect False Modesty

Bluster, arrogance, noise and commotion do not build confidence. Boisterous, boastful behavior is a turn-off to everyone seeking a reasonable answer or practical solution. On the other hand, quiet, calm, thoughtful people who are concentrating on you and your situation are perceived to be genuine and consistently helpful.

Humble people stand out not because they attract attention to themselves, but because they shine the spotlight on others.

- **They understand that giving credit where it is deserved is a motivator for future performance.**
- **They get the satisfaction they need from sharing.**
- **They have learned that modesty attracts and vanity repels.**
- **They understand that compassion establishes more lasting relationships than self-centered acts.**

- **They have learned how to detect false modesty by examining actual behavior not just words.**
- **They get as much gratification from helping others improve as from their own advancement.**
- **They put results above fanfare.**
- **They apologize when they are wrong.**
- **They look for unmet needs.**

The quiet dignity of humble people shines through as an inspiration because:

- **They understand that giving credit where it is deserved is a motivator for future performance**.

> Trust least those
> who claim credit for the
> accomplishments of others.

Johnny Unitas (1933-2002) was known as one of the most reliable quarterbacks in the NFL. That is, of course, if you don't count his very first pass in the league. It was intercepted and run all the way back for a touchdown. When he retired in 1973, he held 22 career passing records and was the first quarterback to throw for 40,000 yards in a career.

Unitas gave credit to everyone who helped and encouraged him along the way. When inducted into the Hall of Fame in 1979, he said, "A man never gets to this station in life without being helped, aided, shoved, pushed and prodded to do better."

Despite all his name recognition and legendary status, Unitas maintained a humble attitude. At his funeral, the Cardinal of Baltimore summarized everyone's feeling. "Johnny," he said, "was the kind of person who would shake hands with a destitute, homeless person and genuinely tell that person that he was honored to meet him."

- **They get the satisfaction they need from sharing.**

Albert Schweitzer (1875-1965) had the talent of many men. First, he acquired two doctoral degrees, in philosophy and theology. He became a pastor and a professor, but also studied music. He played concert organ, piano and mastered organ building. He also wrote one of the best biographies of Johann Sebastian Bach.

All of these accomplishments were achieved before he turned 30. Then he changed direction. He went back to school to study medicine, became an MD, and spent the next 60 years of his life as a healing helper. His zeal and commitment never faltered.

When Schweitzer learned about the dismal conditions in the French colony of Lambarene in Gabon, Africa, he decided he must go there. He left in 1913 with his wife, Helene, and opened his office. That was home for the next 50 years. Life was not easy. He got little sleep and started his work at dawn every day. Individual patient care was foremost, from morning to night.

Albert Einstein, a personal friend, said of Schweitzer, "He did not preach and did not dream that his example would bring comfort to innumerable people. He simply acted out of inner necessity." He dedicated his entire 90 years to the benefit of people in need by living his conviction that, "Example is not the *main* thing in influencing others. It's the *only* thing."

> To be unhappy is a choice
> not a condition.

John Wood is not a well-known name. At only 38 years of age, he left Microsoft after attaining a position as director of business development for China. In that job he learned that over 850 million people in the world are illiterate. That fact prompted him to start "Room to Read," a not-for-profit corporation funding schools and libraries which help Asian children learn to read. His goal is that 10 million of them become literate by 2010.

It won't be easy, but in just 3 years, Room to Read has started 300 school libraries, built 25 schools, donated well over 100,000 books and provided more than 10 computer rooms. Nepal has been the focus of much of the work, but they've already started in Vietnam, and plan to continue their work in India and Cambodia.

Although extremely successful at Microsoft, Wood began to question whether that was enough to make him feel fulfilled. He had 70 people reporting to him, and was well-off financially, due to his stock options.

At his new company, he doesn't even take a salary. In fact, there's only one paid employee, the executive director, who does fundraising and grant writing. Wood knows that even though they've helped 100,000 kids, that's still only 1/100 of 1% of those who need to learn. He knows there's lots of hard work ahead, but he's ready to keep doing it.

- **They have learned that modesty attracts and vanity repels.**

Robert Frost, (1874-1963), one of the best 20th century American poets was "driven" in pursuit of his goal. He wanted to be self-reliant, so turned down an offer of financial help from his grandfather, because it was conditional and expected success within one year. He predicted it would take him 20 years to become recognized as a poet, and it did. *A Boy's Will*, his first book of poetry, was published in 1913. The reviews were not glowing, but he wasn't discouraged.

Frost attended both Dartmouth and Harvard, but graduated from neither. He believed true learning lasted a lifetime, and was not measured by college degrees. He was a slow and deliberate writer, who could spend ten years or more on one poem, reworking it until he was satisfied that it was print-worthy.

Robert Frost won four Pulitzer Prizes, was elected to the Academy of Arts and Letters, and received the Congressional Gold Medal, but never forgot where he came from. He returned to the farm to work, delivering produce orders to a local restaurant, where he was instructed to use the delivery entrance. Never insulted, never arrogant, he needed no fanfare to do what he did best.

- **They understand that compassion establishes more lasting relationships than self-centered acts.**

If there is a line between us,
I will erase it.

Hospital employee Donna Marasco was battling myelogenous leukemia in 2001. Suddenly, she was surrounded by people who gave her their time, love, and even fundraising talents to help her through it.

Since she felt it would be impossible to pay back those who helped her, she is paying it forward instead. She's planning a fundraiser for a friend of her daughter, who was twice hospitalized for spontaneous lung collapse. He was left immobilized and could not work, while the bills continued to mount.

Marasco wants to pass on the generosity and support she received to those who now need it more than she. Unfortunately, she could not attend the fundraiser herself, because her sister in Colorado was undergoing cancer surgery at that same time.

Johnny Weissmuller (1904-1984) was immortalized in his role as Tarzan, playing in 12 Hollywood movies. But did you know he was also one of the best swimmers ever? He won three gold medals and a bronze in the 1924 Olympics and again won two golds in the 1928 Olympic games.

Weissmuller's swimming excellence was not reserved for competition, however. He willingly risked his life in 1927, when a severe storm struck, causing a pleasure boat to capsize in Lake Michigan. Many upper-deck passengers fell overboard. Weissmuller and his brother Peter sprung into action and rowed out to help the accident victims. Johnny kept diving into the treacherous waters rescuing victims, while Peter resuscitated them. The two brothers managed to save 11 people's lives that day, and later received an award for heroism from the city of Chicago. That act of compassion was more meaningful than being inducted into the International Swimming Hall of Fame in 1965.

- **They have learned how to detect false modesty by examining actual behavior not just words.**

> The best time to judge leaders is when they are not on the stage.

Henry (Hank) Aaron believed in constant self-improvement. He never rested on past accomplishments and finally surpassed Babe Ruth's long-standing record as Major League Baseball's all-time home run leader with 755. He also holds the record for runs batted in, with 2,297, and total bases of 6,856. In fact, Aaron holds more batting records than any other player in baseball's history. He was inducted into the National Baseball Hall of Fame in 1982, and named to the Major League Baseball All-Century team in 1999.

Aaron's humility is based upon lessons learned from his parents: 1) always respect whoever you deal with, and 2) give credit wherever it is due. The bottom line he says is, "If you start taking your opponents lightly, that's when you're going to get into some serious trouble."

- **They get as much gratification from helping others improve as from their own advancement.**

> Those who are poor and beg become losers.
> Those who are poor and work become winners.

Jack Northrup (1895-1981) never graduated from college. In fact, he didn't even attend. He decided on aviation as a career at age 16, and shortly after high school, got into the airplane business. He founded Northrup Aircraft Co. in 1939. Unencumbered by conventional thought, he began designing aircraft. Though recognized as a leader, he realized what he didn't know, and studied hard.

Northrup would never take credit for his employees' work. Rather, he made sure they got the patents they deserved. He encouraged engineers to think for themselves, and not bring him problems without also recommending at least one possible solution. He designed the "Flying Wing," which was a forerunner of today's stealth bombers.

He also used his inventiveness to meet other needs. In 1946, he could see the limited choices returning WWII veterans had for prostheses. Soon, he and his staff created lightweight limbs exceeding anything else available at the time. Refusing to accept any money for his work, he assigned the patents to leading prosthesis firms, so they could develop even better products.

Mia Hamm is probably the best known female athlete in the U.S. She has been a member of the U.S. World Cup Soccer team for 16 years (starting when she was only 15) and the star player most of that time. But Hamm prefers to defer to others on the team and back away from the attention she gets as her sport's top attraction. She wants to avoid taking credit away from her teammates and they frequently step in to protect her when she has trouble getting the privacy she wants. She usually defers to the team's spokespersons, Julie Foudy or Brandi Chastain.

Says Hamm, "I don't say I'm the best because I don't think it. I look at myself as I did when I was a scared kid growing up trying to fit in, just trying to make it."

Mia wants to help her team win and it shows. Her underlying belief that she can always do better is reflected in her unparalleled career, which includes winning four NCAA championships at the University of North Carolina, two World

Cups and an Olympic Gold medal. She has also broken the international scoring record for men and women.

Not bad for a lady who is happy when team members get attention instead of her.

- **They put results above fanfare.**

> Belief with no action is
> a sail with no wind.

Edwin Land (1909-1991) graduated from the Norwich Free Academy with honors, but dropped out of Harvard in his freshman year. He preferred to study on his own at the local public library. His lack of a degree didn't stop him from being second only to the renowned Thomas Alva Edison in the number of U.S. patents held.

Well known for inventing Polaroid cameras and instant film, he also created high-speed and X-ray film, ID systems, 3-D and instant movie cameras, and devices for night vision and aerial reconnaissance. Many of his inventions met the needs of the U.S. Government, such as infrared polarizers, night-adaptation goggles and an optical surveillance system. Others have more common applications, including the Liquid Crystal Display (LCD), and glare-free headlights.

Land hoped that his work would prove useful. He took his company from a small basement concern to the heights of a firm employing thousands of people around the world for over 50 years.

When asked about retiring, he made his outlook toward work very clear, "What I want is not retirement but more years."

Roy Boehm created the first U.S. Navy SEAL (SeaAirLand) team and training program. The job required tremendous focus. He refused to let anything stop him, and directed all his energy into making it a reality. He had to cut through miles of red-tape and many bureaucrats, and didn't worry about embarrassing them. He knew it could be his undoing, but believed the team would survive.

Boehm's motto lives on with the SEALS, "If you always tell the truth, you never have to worry about what you said." His loyalty to his men was reciprocated by their commitment to "march through hell with him."

- **They apologize when they are wrong.**

Setbacks endured are
pathways to growth.

Beverly Engel, author of *The Power of Apology: Healing Steps to Transform All Your Relationships*, says: "Apologizing when we have made a mistake or committed an oversight conveys a message of regret and concern on our part and an acknowledgment that the other person has a right to be upset."

- **They look for unmet needs.**

Dr. Darrel Carter practices medicine off the beaten path. There are only about 18,000 people in the scattered towns and rural areas around Granite Falls, Minnesota, where he lives. Alarmed by the lack of care available in small towns, he set about to narrow the gap. For 3 years and thousands of hours, he tirelessly led over 20 other health professionals to establish the Comprehensive Advanced Life Support (CALS) system. This course for rural doctors, nurses and volunteers in basic emergency care has trained over 1300 people since 1996. The 1,000 page manual could become the basis for a national program.

But Carter keeps on volunteering even after going through kidney cancer and surgery 5 years ago. That experience, he says, helped him communicate better with his patients. Most fittingly, the humble, modest, generous Dr. Darrel Carter was named the American Academy of Family Physicians' Man of the Year for 2003.

7

Random Acts of Kindness

Few human beings, if any, can ignore kindness. Something in our makeup seeks it and appreciates it. The people we admire most seem to be kind and thoughtful most of the time. When a stranger needs help they help them. When a friend needs sympathy they give it. When a child needs encouragement, they provide it.

The irony is we are not born instinctively kind or even gentle. On the contrary, infants and small children are naturally self-centered and quick tempered. We must learn about kindness from exemplary people who touch our lives and the earlier the better.

Nothing to Gain

Humble adults are consistently kind because they feel they have nothing to gain by aggressiveness and selfishness. They find happiness in simple, little things:

- appreciating the day
- laughing at themselves
- mentoring a child
- listening to an old person
- preventing another's mistake
- holding a hand they love
- escaping an injury
- seeing their advice work
- seeing loved ones smile

— being consulted
— being accepted
— being appreciated

> Happiness is a process,
> not a thing.
>
> —Gerald Edelman, writer

When humility prevails, kindness is not a rational or logical act. It is instinctive, spontaneous and heartfelt. The personal, social or political consequences are not considered. What matters is, did we do the right thing and was it helpful?

Humble people do not perform acts of kindness according to a plan. They do them when they are needed whenever that may be. "Make a Difference Day" has offered people across the country the opportunity to do just that. For example, Miriam Ortiz, who recently moved to the U.S. from Mexico, organized 180 of her neighbors to rehab 12 homes in her town. Volunteers cleaned and pressure-washed five homes, painted four, cleaned two yards, replaced windows, repaired screens, removed 582 bags of trash and planted a garden. What a difference a day made!

Food on Foot is another example. They feed as many as 84,300 homeless people in Los Angeles. Besides food, they give people anything helpful: bus tickets, a pair of warm socks, a bicycle or a wheelchair. When asked what they needed, most people requested simple things that we take for granted.

Jim and Judy Huff, who are disabled, wanted to repay the caring they received from others. They decided to donate warm winter coats to a non-profit organization. But they wanted to keep it secret, so they called to make sure it would be open on October 26, when they delivered 162 coats plus matching gloves with no fanfare. That's how they wanted it, because Judy says she learned early that boasting was a no-no. She was afraid she'd "lose the blessing from it."

Why is it easier for some people to be kind without thinking about it?

- **They believe they can get ahead even when they step aside.**
- **They are not dejected when not in the limelight.**
- **They get satisfaction from responding to others' needs.**
- **Though disappointed, they bounce back.**
- **They don't interpret failure as permanent.**
- **They look for situations where they can make a difference.**
- **They sense when others need them most.**

Humble people see kindness as its own reward because:

- **They believe they can get ahead even when they step aside.**

At age 93, Benny Carter, jazz saxophonist, band leader, composer and arranger is still working, or maybe we should say "playing."

Duke Ellington believed that Carter's contribution "is so tremendous it completely fazes me." Quite a compliment from Duke, one of the most prolific American composers of all time. Yet, Benny remains totally down to earth. His humility is obvious. Everyone thinks of him as "the nicest guy you ever want to meet."

Carter says he wants to get along with everyone, and he's honored when they want to do the same. When playing with younger musicians (and few aren't) he tries to show them he values what they do, and that helps them perform even better.

In a career that's lasted more than 70 years, he's written arrangements for Benny Goodman, Glenn Miller, and many other great band leaders. He also broke through the race-barrier in Hollywood, by becoming one of the first African-Americans to compose musical scores for movie sound tracks.

It's hard to believe that Chuck Noll didn't put winning first. He's fifth in all-time NFL wins, the only coach whose team won four Super Bowls, in 1974, '75, '78 and '79. The fact that he led the Pittsburgh Steelers to nine division titles and 15 winning seasons in his 23 year career helped him into the Pro Football Hall of Fame in 1993.

But Noll put teaching above all. He knew that if he could do a good job teaching, winning would follow. He aimed to find good young players, with unlimited potential and help them rise to stardom. He never felt he could begin to coast, because: "the only place you coast is downhill."

Noll concentrated on coaching and kept a low profile. He didn't want the spotlight on himself to distract his players. His humility was the background for his team's success.

- **They are not dejected when not in the limelight.**

Neil Armstrong was a test pilot, flew 78 Korean War combat missions, became an astronaut, served as commander of the Gemini 8 space flight, then of the Apollo 11 moon mission in 1969.

As the first man to walk on the moon, it would have been easy to capitalize on that fame, but he chose not to. He avoided the celebrity of his moon walk, because he felt it was absolutely a team effort. He credits all the behind-the-scenes workers at NASA who made it possible. He insists it could have been anyone at that moment, but it just happened to be him.

Armstrong always believed in doing the best job he could do. His motto: "There's no need to publicize yourself—your work will do it for you."

- **They get satisfaction from responding to others' needs.**

> Sincerity is measured by
> 3 words—"Count on me."

One of the best ways to detect humility is to see who responds quickest to emergency or crisis situations. The 9/11/01 disaster at the World Trade Center in New York City provided many examples.

Brian Clark was on the 84th floor of the South Tower at 8:45 when he heard a great roar and saw a huge fireball. People were jumping out of windows all around him. Dazed and horrified, he couldn't bear to watch them.

Regaining his senses, he gathered six people and worked his way toward a stairwell. A few moments later, on the 81st floor he heard a voice calling, "Help me, I can't breathe."

Brian instinctively shouted, "Hang on," then noticed that the voice was coming from behind a huge wall. At the bottom he saw a stretched-out hand, and heard a pounding. Together, they expanded the hole until Stanley Praimnath could be pulled through. "I'm Stanley," he said to Brian, "and you are my brother for life!"

No one pushed Brian or even suggested that he rescue Stanley on that horrible day. Even now, he doesn't know how he tolerated the searing heat and flames, the choking dust, the total darkness, the shock or the pain. What he does know is that he is thankful for the opportunity to save the life of a stranger.

Another unsung hero from September 11th was firefighter Dave Fontana. Fontana helped people every day; helping was his life's mission. He didn't let anything block that path.

One of seven children, he learned to share early in life. Kids loved Dave. And Dave just loved his kid. His wife was afraid he'd wake his son Aidan, because he kept whispering "I love you" gently and repeatedly to him

Fontana's eighth wedding anniversary was Sept. 11th, 2001. He switched shifts so he could meet his wife Marian at 9:00 Tuesday morning. She was waiting for him at a coffee shop, but he never showed up. A five alarmer reached his squad right at the change of shift. The first plane had just struck Tower One of the World Trade Center. Although his shift had ended, Fontana jumped on the truck for the last time.

Dave's wife Marian hopes others will use his life as an example. She urges people not to hold grudges, or stay angry.

- **Though disappointed, they bounce back.**

> You can't change what's over.
> Move on.

Thomas Monaghan was not afraid to work. He had 44 different jobs until the time he enlisted in the Marines. After his discharge, he and his brother took a loan for just under $1,000 to buy a very small pizza parlor. They worked it together for a while, until he sold his VW and bought his brother's half. Working seven days a week, and over 100 hours, was common.

Monaghan always wanted to keep his managers on their toes, so he used quarterly instead of annual reviews. To discourage managers from acting out of their own self-interest, he imposed fines when they would say "I" or "my" instead of "we" or "our." That helped stop turf wars. He also made it possible for employees to "earn" a Domino's franchise by working their way up.

Monaghan's management style worked. The Domino's pizza chain now has more than 6,000 stores in 60 countries, with sales topping $2 billion a year.

Making money is no longer Tom Monaghan's main priority. Faith has played a large role in his life since his childhood. In 1998, he sold his 93% stake for $1 billion, and is now engaged full time in religious philanthropic work.

- **They don't interpret failure as permanent.**

Success is not avoiding failure, it is believing that failure is not a permanent condition. Marco Quinones, a Mexican agronomist, knows that. He lives in Ethiopia, where he has trained over 50,000 farmers with tiny plots of land, how to triple (or more) their basic food production. They grew mostly corn. Before he came, they were only producing half the grain needed to survive. Dependent on foreign imports many starved.

Now Ethiopia has more than doubled its grain production and also produces enough corn to have a surplus, which it exports to neighboring countries.

Another is Dr. Don Hopkins, who specializes in rare diseases. The effects of one of them, known as Guinea worm, are indescribably ugly. It infects poor, isolated people, mainly in Africa, India, Pakistan and Yemen. Dr. Hopkins goes into the villages, talks with people, teaches them what they must know about the causes and prevention. In 1987, there were approximately three and a half million people with Guinea worm. Just 10 short years later, that number had been reduced to 130,000, due in large part to Dr. Don Hopkins' efforts.

- **They look for situations where they can make a difference.**

> Happiness doesn't
> depend upon who you are
> or what you have. It depends
> solely on what you think.
>
> —Dale Carnegie, writer

15-year-old Matthew Brown took on a project to fix up a playground for abused children at the Community Hope Center in Cottage Hills, Illinois. It was to help him become an Eagle Scout, but many children benefited. He spent 400 hours repainting and refurbishing donated playground equipment, and soliciting donations for the paint and ground cover worth $8,500. He then recruited 17 other volunteers, including some Boy Scouts to help. Tell me, would you like to hire this young man?

Nurse Marilyn Emmett and 17 volunteers from a hospital emergency room helped a 78-year-old Wolcottville, IL woman after her leg was amputated. The volunteers built a ramp at her home, so she could enter her house in her wheelchair. ER nurse Marilyn Emmett said she was ecstatic. Would you like to have any one of these volunteers as a friend?

Fabiola Scholnick was still grieving the death of her two sons, Jeremy, 17, and Jonathan, 14, as a result of a car accident. Both her sons had donated time to helping the homeless, so she decided to honor their memories by doing the same. She recruited 22 volunteers, 14 of them teens. They raised $1,400 and collected over 40 boxes of food and toiletries, which was given to over 1,000 homeless people. I ask you, who do you think benefited most—the volunteers or the homeless people?

At age 94, Eleanor Reed thought she might be a "burden" on an organization that requested she join them. They refused to accept her "excuse," so she became a member.

That was 3 years ago. Since then she has chaired committees, hand-knit items for the Bazaar, attended most meetings, baked for fundraising events, and recently presented a great book review. When someone comes home from the hospital, Eleanor brings them home-cooked food, and of course, her smile. Although she has endured several back operations, and recently had a kidney removed, she appreciates her good health by crediting her activities and "her morning bran muffin."

Now, no other member would be missed as much as Eleanor.

- **They sense when others need them most.**

Raising five sons alone after her husband died was only the beginning of sacrifices made by Cathy Darin. Some friends call her "the Queen of Grief." For 13 years Cathy has served as grief counselor for St. Raphael's Catholic Church in Naperville, Illinois and chaplain for the local Police Department and Edward Hospital.

Hundreds of families have been comforted by her as they dealt with illness, emergencies, tragedy or death. Now the situation is reversed as Cathy is fighting a personal battle with thyroid cancer, which has been diagnosed as terminal. Friends gather frequently for church services, receptions and home parties to honor her. At a recent event her son Tom paid Cathy the ultimate compliment, "My mom's given her life to others. Now I'm asking her advice on how I'm going to deal with her illness."

Kindness is not intended to be repayable. It is instinctive with humble people. They see it as benefiting them, more than those they help. And, sooner or later, it always does.

Defining Moments

The building blocks of life are both inherited and acquired. The mortar, however, which keeps us standing is revealed in those events when our choices establish our identity.

Looking back we realize that many of life's most precious times went unnoticed. Yet these "defining moments" are perhaps the best indicators of who we are and what we want to be.

The ups and downs in my life have convinced me that we bring out our best in 7 major circumstances:

- When we focus on basic needs.
- When we put someone else ahead of ourselves.
- When we take responsibility.
- When we are accountable for our actions.
- When we choose truth over deception.
- When credit is shared.
- When we must start over.

Consider these examples:

- **When we focus on basic needs.**

Henry Morrison Flagler (1830-1913) was ever the optimist. That attitude took him from earning $5 a month as a store clerk to co-founding Standard Oil and finally to becoming a visionary developer of uninhabitable swampland in what is now Florida.

Not your typical successful businessman type, Flagler was the son of a minister. He left home at only 14, after finishing eighth grade. His natural gift for sales, combined with lots of hard work, helped him get raises and promotions.

Flagler succeeded, but constantly sought out new opportunities. He learned that salt had been discovered in Michigan, and was desperately needed to preserve Army rations during the Civil War. That prompted him to invest his entire net worth of $50,000 in the salt business. When the war ended, however, the demand and prices fell, destroying his company. Flagler returned to Ohio, so poor, he skipped lunches in order to save money, but he repaid the $50,000 loan plus interest.

On doctor's orders, Flagler took his wife from Cleveland to the warmer climate of Florida. Largely undeveloped in the 1870's, he saw great possibilities, while others saw only swampland. He built hotels, hospitals, and unified transportation systems, including the Florida East Coast Railway. At that time, Dade County, an area of more than 7,200 square miles, had a population of only 720.

With his many contributions, Flagler remained humble. Building offered him challenges and thrills, rather than fame and fortune. The residents of one of his communities wanted to name it Flagler, after him, but he insisted they choose the area's original Native American name instead—Miami.

Richard Avedon reported that when the terrorist plane

hit Tower One of the World Trade Center on September 11, Michael Hingson was at his desk on the 78ᵗʰ floor. His friend Roselle was nearby. Calmly, Roselle led Michael and Michael led his colleagues down to the ground floor. But safety was still miles away. As they made it outside, Tower Two collapsed and in the smoke and rubble, Roselle led Michael and Michael led those who fled—all the way to the river. Michael has been blind since birth. Roselle is his guide dog.

"We're a team," Michael says again and again. And so they are.

> Honesty is matching
> reputation with reality.

Possum Trot, Texas is home to only 300 families, mostly African American, who live in modest homes. The local church's pastor, Reverend W.C. Martin struggles to keep it afloat. Although Martin and his wife, Donna already had two children, they decided to adopt others who'd been beaten, neglected, abused, or worse. They have brought four into their home. Not without problems, of course—lying and stealing meant survival where these kids came from.

Donna Martin asked Susan Ramsey, a social worker from the adoption agency if she would come to the church to tell others about the opportunities to adopt. Although the families were poor, they seemed willing to share what they had with these children. And they did. All were kids who had been molested, who had to scrape for food, some had never heard the words *I love you*. Ramsey matched them up with single mothers, middle-aged couples with their own brood to raise, older adults with grown children, even four sisters, who took in eleven kids.

And Possum Trot kept taking in children. By the end of the summer of 2001, 61 children had been adopted.

- ## When we put someone else ahead of ourselves.

The heroes of United Airlines Flight 93 prevented a terrorist attack on Washington D.C. on 9/11/01. They probably saved the U.S. Capitol or the White House. The terrorists who planned attacks on both targets, along with the World Trade Center and the Pentagon that day, would have likely hit all their targets, if a few determined passengers had not fought back.

Todd Beamer seemed to most people to be an ordinary guy, who was especially devoted to his family. Jeremy Glick was a black belt, and competed in the NCAA Judo Championships, even though he had no coach and no team. He won the national title in 1993. Mark Bingham founded and was president of the Mark Bingham Group, a San Fransisco public relations firm. He took people under his wing and mentored them in public relations. Thomas Burnett was a problem solver. When he put his mind to a problem, he would find a solution.

These four men were strangers to each other when they boarded Flight 93. At 9:58 a.m. the four rallied the other passengers. Action was absolutely necessary. "Are you ready?" Beamer asked. "Let's roll." Together, these people fought back in the war on terrorism to defend liberty. The terrorists didn't know what hit them. These Americans would not be pushed around.

Larry Miller's family had worked the same 2,300 acres of Midwest farmland since the 1700's. They couldn't afford to hire any help, so it was always a family affair. This year's crop was bountiful. Larry's son Jerry and his wife Jennifer had their first child, a baby boy named Brody. Everyone was ecstatic.

But by late August, Brody was very ill. He had a rare disease—hemangioma. Jennifer stayed with him at the hospital in St. Louis. Jerry stayed behind and worked the fields with his dad until the end of October, but then was needed at the hospital too. Larry encouraged him to go.

Larry continued to work as fast as he could, because the corn and soybeans would rot if not picked soon. At that point, with almost no time left, and 800 acres to go, Larry was concerned. He'd never hesitate to lend a hand to someone in need. His only problem was learning to accept help.

His neighbors insisted, however, and together they finished quickly. He wondered aloud how he could ever repay them. "You already have," they told him. At Thanksgiving that year, they thanked God for the return of Brody's health, for another year of living off the land, and for the fact that when you reach out and give to another, your arms are also open to receive.

- **When we take responsibility.**

Bill Nelson took building maintenance to new heights in Chicago Heights public schools. He initiated steps leading to donation of 500 slightly used seats from the Marcus Cinema. The school did not have funds for a major update, so when Nelson observed dozens of seats in storage, he talked to the theater manager about them. The theater was glad to give them to the public school. The school funded the rest of the renovation, and the maintenance crew, led by Nelson, did most of the work. No one pushed or prodded him. He just saw a need and met it!

If we think about it, everyone has a recollection of unselfishness which stays in our mind and never goes away. Writer Mary Schmich remembered the story about her Aunt Christine who died recently at age 92. Her family thought for years that she loved chicken necks because whenever chicken was served she always took the neck. That was during the depression. Later, when asked why, she said she "hated it, but when they had only one chicken and a lot of people to share it, she realized somebody had to eat the neck. So she decided she would and tell everybody she liked it. Needless to say, Aunt Christine had a tremendous influence on a lot of people for a long, long time.

- **When we are accountable for our actions.**

It was 1960. Just one month into her new position as medical officer, Dr. Frances Kelsey, age 41, was assigned to test the drug thalidomide for FDA approval. Everyone expected it to sail through the process quickly. But she was concerned with the clinical results submitted by the company. She felt it was more like anecdotal evidence than a well-designed clinical study. Therefore, Kelsey refused approval for distribution here.

That refusal spared thousands in the U.S. from having babies with severe birth defects, such as occurred in countries where the drug was approved. It also earned her international recognition.

It wasn't easy standing up to the powerful drug company. When she would not change her stance, the pharmaceutical rep complained to her higher-ups that Kelsey was being unreasonable, and wasting valuable time. They were very anxious to get this drug to the U.S. market.

But Kelsey wouldn't budge. She continued to demand more and better clinical data, further slowing the application process. She realized that the drug could pass through the placenta from mother to child, which was confirmed by a German doctor. The drug was then pulled in other countries, but too late. More than 10,000 babies in 46 countries had birth defects from thalidomide.

It was with humility and a desire to serve that she accepted the President's Award for Distinguished Federal Civilian Service, the highest civilian honor in 1962. She was also inducted into the National Women's Hall of Fame in Seneca Falls, NY in 2000.

- **When we choose truth over deception.**

> Beware those who adjust
> the 10 Commandments to
> suit their purposes.

When he graduated from high school, Ron Santo was considered the best baseball prospect in the state of Washington. He signed a pro contract at the age of 18, in 1959. Right before leaving home, he had a physical exam. His urine test came back with sugar in it, a warning sign for diabetes. Of course, he wanted to know if he could still play baseball. His doctor doubted that he'd make it through his first minor league season. But Ron knew his determination to play in the big leagues would carry him through.

Santo discovered that the long-term effects of diabetes could be devastating and the average life expectancy after diagnosis is only twenty-five years. He was afraid he might die by age 43, but was convinced that with diet and proper exercise, he would survive. Between innings, if his blood-sugar levels dipped, he'd drink some orange juice, or eat a candy bar.

In June 1960, the Cubs took Ron Santo up to the majors. He secretly took his insulin injections, afraid that if the team found out, they might send him back to the minors, or even release him. Since glucose-measuring devices were still primitive, he was afraid of slipping into a diabetic coma.

In 1963, Santo made the all-star team and was named Cubs team captain. At that point, he felt he had to tell his coaches and teammates. He gave them details, but asked that it not leave the room. Not until 1971 did the public learn about his illness. When the team decided to honor him with a special Ron Santo Day, he asked that donations go to the Juvenile Diabetes Foundation.

Santo is a role-model for diabetes sufferers, and the annual walks in his name raise many millions for research. His health remained good until age 60, when he had to have several operations, and circulatory problems necessitated amputation of both his legs. Ron Santo's life is a neon sign reading, "Don't stop using your God-given gifts and talents. Follow your dreams."

- **When credit is shared.**

> Most everything I've done
> I've copied from someone else.
>
> —Sam Walton, founder Wal-Mart

One of the best-ever examples of the benefits of sharing credit is the 2003 NBA Champion San Antonio Spurs. David Robinson, the long-time star of the team welcomed Tim Duncan several years before as the new leading scorer, rebounder and most publicized player. The Spurs faced potential internal conflicts in their own locker room, not in the press.

Sub Steve Kerr owns 5 NBA Championship rings after 15 seasons, and is the league's all-time 3 point percentage shooter. Many believe he will soon be a pro head coach. Kerr calls Duncan unselfish and "unbelievably humble."

Robinson, a gentleman on and off the court, is a graduate of the U.S. Naval Academy. He put off his pro career to meet his military obligation and recently donated $10 million to build a school in San Antonio for disadvantaged children. He was recently inducted into the World Sports Humanitarian Hall of Fame.

When praised by fans and teammates for his shooting under pressure, Kerr is honest about his role. "I have people ahead of me who are better players than I am," he says. "If they need me, I'll be ready." That's how trust is earned, and winning organizations are built.

- **When we must start over.**

John Madden is one of the best known names in football. His 103-32-7 regular season coaching record in 10 seasons with the Raiders is second only to Vince Lombardi. He also got to 100 wins faster than any other coach in NFL history.

Madden's own career as a player ended with an injury in training camp during his rookie year with the Eagles. Instead of just packing it in, he spent a lot of time with Norm Van Brocklin, the great quarterback, to learn intricacies he might later apply to coaching. The two met frequently during the 1959 season and Madden watched, listened and learned.

Madden took several lower-level coaching positions to build his knowledge base. He knew that experience is the best teacher. He coached college teams before becoming an assistant with the Raiders in 1967. In 1969, at just 32, he became the youngest head coach ever in the old American Football League.

Jim and Mary Lou Beers may not be your typical happily married couple, but they are extraordinarily happy and in love. Married since 1964, the romance still thrives, in spite of extremely difficult circumstances. They had 2 daughters, and Mary Lou was pregnant with the third, when in her seventh month, she fell down some stairs, broke both legs and needed long bed rest. Her total helplessness and dependence on Jim made her realize how grateful she was that he rose to the task.

In 1971, Mary Lou was again pregnant, when Jim left on a sales call and ended up in a hospital emergency room. He had a stroke and was found collapsed in his car on the side of the highway. Two years later, during surgery, he had another massive stroke. Almost totally paralyzed, and on life support for three months, they finally found a way to communicate with hand signals. It was a year before he could come home. His 6 foot 5 inch, 220-pound body, now down to only 85 pounds.

Jim needed round-the-clock care, which Mary Lou provided. The kids felt neglected at times, but they now understand it. His only son, Jimmy, now a club PGA golf pro, jokes, "My dad was the perfect father—the only one who never yelled when his kid was up at bat." By 1975, Jim wanted to be the good, loving husband his wife deserved, and Mary Lou was definitely ready for some relief. Dining out more often proved to be challenging, but pleasant. Traveling was difficult, but they did it anyway. Then, something else surprised everyone, including themselves—Mary Lou became pregnant with their fifth child.

The Beers' message is "Love can endure all things. Marriage and commitment go way beyond the easy days of youth and health." Mary Lou tells young people to look beyond the superficial appearances of people, see the person inside, and love and accept them for who they are.

Recently, Mary Lou's high school inducted her into its hall of fame, and Jim introduced her at the ceremony with these words: "If I tried to tell you all she is to me, it would take a lifetime." Looking lovingly at his wife, he lifted a single red rose slightly and said, "Mary Lou, this bud's for you. I love you."

No Need to Get Even

Humble People Don't Have to Watch Their Back

The urge to get even is self-defeating. It compels us to spend time punishing others instead of improving ourselves. It makes us defensive, antagonistic and resented. It provides untold reasons for people to resist our conclusions and recommendations. It stops us from being an effective team member. It blocks the path to advancement. It blinds us from seeing the good in people and the positive side of controversial issues.

> You can't motivate
> people by lighting
> a fire under them,
> you have to light
> a fire within them.

Humble people can move forward without handicapping themselves with either self-pity or vengeance because:

- They are sensitive to hardship.
- They respect different talents.
- They acknowledge their vulnerability.
- They recognize others' abilities.
- They are protected by those they help.
- They are trusted.
- They tolerate rejection.
- They expand their skills.

Humble people are better able to understand others' needs because:

- **They are sensitive to hardship.**

Dorothea Dix (1802-1887) could have spent her life bitterly opposing the discrimination she faced as a woman. The fact that she could not own property, vote or even enter the Chambers of legislative buildings did not keep her from devoting her life to others. Her relentless energy and perseverance is unsurpassed in establishing humane treatment for the mentally ill.

Influenced first by the preaching of her father who was a Methodist minister, her wealthy grandmother provided tutors to prepare her for teaching. At age 14 she persuaded her grandmother to pay for a free school for poor children. Dix recorded the successful methods she used and that manual helped so many people it was printed for 70 years.

After her work with poverty-stricken children, at age 34, she became concerned about the plight of mentally ill adults. In those days, people who could not be cared for at home were kept in almshouses or jail. Typically chained or locked in cells or cages, they were often without heat and victimized by the criminals with whom they were housed. Unable, as a woman, to enter the Massachusetts Legislature Chambers herself, she contacted members individually detailing the horrible conditions she had discovered. Her words were powerful, "I come to place before the Legislature of Massachusetts the condition of the miserable, the desolate, the outcast . . . If I inflict pain upon you, and move you to horror, it is to acquaint you with the suffering which you have the power to alleviate, and make you hasten to the relief of the victims of legalized barbarity."

She lived to see one federal and 32 state humane asylums opened and more than 100 followed. Because she became well known in Washington D.C., she was selected to be supervisor of women nurses for the military during the Civil War.

- **They respect different talents.**

Mel Renfro didn't have much growing up. Even now, he makes the most of his abilities by helping children who come from poverty. In fact, he donates his time to some 20 charities. Sports were Renfro's ladder to climb up from his economic circumstances. He went all out in track and football since his youth. By high school, he was up for All-City and All-State awards. He was already becoming well known.

But he continued to be humble. He knows everyone has different talents, and he recognizes his, but doesn't think it makes him better than anyone else. Renfro was chosen All-American in college football in 1961, '62 and '63. As a pro, he played for the Dallas Cowboys from 1964-'77. He made it into 10 NFL Pro Bowls, was chosen as an All-Pro defensive back four times, and was inducted into the NFL Hall of Fame in 1996. Renfro's conclusion: "Sometimes, when you're pushed further than you've ever gone before, you realize you can accomplish things you never thought possible."

- **They acknowledge their vulnerability.**

> Admitting a mistake
> *defines*.
> Not admitting a mistake
> *denies*.
> Lying about a mistake
> ***destroys***.

Harriet Rubin learned a lot from adman Jay Chiat. He shared his secret for getting protected people to take his calls. He calls the secretary, says he is "Mr. X's" doctor, and he has the results of his tests. Mr. X inevitably takes the call. Unfortunately, Chiat himself received a similar call, but it was for real. He became one of many powerful people, who learn they are powerless in some circumstance. Rubin's conclusion is that it is useless to try to live life and always be shielded from bad things.

People who seek power lead the toughest lives. Rather than choosing comfort, they overcome obstacles. By examining their lives, and not simply their deeds, you realize they can face pain and loss, because they embrace their fate, and don't run from it. Living to them is an opportunity to accept challenges and overcome them.

- **They recognize others' abilities.**

Andrew Carnegie (1835-1919) came to the U.S. as a penniless Scottish immigrant boy. By age 33, he had become a prosperous businessman, but wanted to accomplish more than just accumulate money. He wanted to be able to create institutions which would help people make the most of themselves.

Carnegie did not want to die with his fortune intact so he set aside a large amount for his family but gave a much larger share to the Carnegie Corp., a foundation he established in 1911, which is still going strong. Funds were provided to create Carnegie Hall, the Carnegie Institute, the Carnegie Hero Fund Commission, Carnegie-Mellon University, and more than 2,800 public libraries. Why? Because Carnegie believed that ignorance is the worst enemy of the poor.

Yet Carnegie avoided credit for his accomplishments. He gave it to the people who helped him. He was convinced that, "You must capture and keep the heart of a man before his brain can do its best." His unselfish convictions were so strong, he wrote his own epitaph. It reads, "Here lies a man who enlisted in his service better men than himself."

- **They are protected by those they help.**

In 1917, Harry Truman was a 33-year-old commander of a rowdy Army reserve unit. He managed to get their support by letting them know he was in charge and would work as hard as they did. They ended up on the front lines in France, fighting World War I together. By the time Germany surrendered, they were recognized as one of the best units in the regiment.

Truman then served as a U.S. senator, vice president then president when Franklin Roosevelt died in 1945. Truman created loyalty among his staff members by genuinely caring for them. They all recognized his compassionate attitude. He personally visited the kitchen to compliment the help.

He was the first senator to receive his own pass key for early morning building access. His motto: "Give it all you've got."

- **They are trusted.**

> Repeating a lie
> will not make it true.

Research shows that humility is a key factor in building trust. Being able to admit doubt or error and acknowledging mistakes, nurtures support. Co-workers then believe, *I can trust you. You won't try to bluff me.* Those rated most trustworthy were also thought to be highly competent. Those who are trusted are seen as a collaborator, not as a competitor.

Admitting your mistakes may be embarrassing, but will improve your reputation in the long run. Often even your toughest critics will be won over when you do not try to cover up because you can then shift focus from the blunder to creating a brighter future. The advantage is that you can move the discussion forward, quickly off the mistake and on to what's next.

We all make mistakes. Acknowledging them leads people to be sympathetic, instead of angry with you for lying, or trying to hide the error. If you admit it and explain concisely what went wrong and why, it's like pulling off a band-aid. If you do it quickly, it will be less painful. Then end on a high note. Move swiftly and sincerely from problem to solution, totally focused on learning from your mistake and using the experience to avoid making it again.

- **They tolerate rejection.**

Baseball pioneer Branch Rickey made a gigantic difference in the game. Because he believed the best players had good moral character both on and off the field, he established a "farm system" of minor leagues to enable him to thoroughly evaluate players' maturity and potential.

After having had many hours to determine Jackie Robinson's ability to withstand insults and racial slurs, Rickey hired him to be the first black player in the Major Leagues. Rickey served as a father figure for Robinson during many years when both were severely criticized daily.

His statement to Robinson capsules his rare combination of humility, friendship and leadership. "There is virtually nobody on our side." He told him. "We can only win if we can convince the world I'm doing this because you're a great ballplayer and a fine gentleman." Robinson was both and Rickey's heritage is unsurpassed.

Columnist Mary Schmich gives this excellent advice: "Remember the compliments, forget the insults."

- **They expand their skills.**

Muhammad Yunus, an economist who returned to his native Bangladesh after he received his Ph.D. in the U.S., realized his teaching was not addressing his country's greatest problem—poverty, hunger and starvation. He strove to understand poor people, and what made them so vulnerable to famine.

Since founding Grameen Bank in 1983, it has dispersed almost $4 billion in loans to 2.6 million people. Remarkably, 98% of all the loans have already been repaid. 5% of all its borrowers rise from poverty each year. Now many countries are copying this model with similar success. He saw how little it took to help some people out of a self-perpetuating situation—for as little as $27, some could change their lives.

Yunus simply took responsibility to make the connection between poor people in villages and a bank. It took seven years of trying before he finally received permission to establish his independent bank, which now has over 1,000 branches, and more than 11,000 employees. By trusting people other banks rejected, and sharing his talents, one man has made an incredible difference in the lives of millions.

> You can enter my mind
> only with my permission.

10

Why Egotists are Lonely

> The egotist's message is always the same, "Hey you, get back in the shadows."

To a certain degree all leaders are ego-driven. They have an urgent desire to move forward to meet needs, to accomplish things. The hazards appear when that need becomes an all-consuming desire to be the center of attention at all times, in all places, under all circumstances. This compulsion can force them into a lifestyle resulting in self-imposed loneliness. They come to believe that they alone are all they need; dependence on others is a sign of weakness; delegated work will always have to be redone; confidence will usually be misplaced.

> Humble people outlast both fads and egotists.

Egotists are lonely because they can never satisfy their need for attention:

- Their selfishness isolates them.
- No one wants to help them.
- Most of their accomplishments are shallow.
- Their vanity drives away possible supporters.
- They won't show appreciation.
- They refuse to be sympathetic.
- They believe admitting mistakes is a sign of weakness.
- Their towering ambition exceeds reality.

Humble people, on the other hand, find satisfaction, and often joy, in attracting attention to the needs of others.

They realize that the effectiveness of egotists is limited because:

- **Their selfishness isolates them.**

Humility is not vanity in disguise. It is the genuine feeling that we both are important, not just me. It is the impulse to ask, to consult, to be helpful. Humble people are instinctively unselfish but they also wisely understand the downside of vanity. They have seen continuing evidence of how "me first" people are left to stand alone. They know the hopeless feeling of asking for volunteers and getting none. They appreciate how much less time it takes three people to do a job than one.

More and more successful business leaders combat possible isolation by using outside advisers to help them evaluate new projects or analyze reasons for poor results. They don't ignore input from employees but seek objective help from people who have no direct stake in the outcome. This is a role

I have been asked to fill in scores of situations for over 30 years. The process has almost always been successful when the client is willing to control egotistic impulses.

Sometimes executives and business owners prevent isolation by using peers in non-competing companies to examine a problem they face. They put their power, authority and ego on the back burner while they get a reality check or fresh perspective. It also sends a powerful message that they don't see their personal views as omnipotent.

Actor Harrison Ford offends many of his movie star contemporaries by referring to his job as a craft, not a skill. He even quit acting for 12 years and became a carpenter so he would "have another way to make a living." He got into acting in the first place, he says, not because he was looking for fame or big money but because he was "no good at anything else." This lack of pretense and reaction to rejection enabled him to persist for 15 years before he could support himself as an actor.

- **No one wants to help them.**

Every problem raises three questions: What must be done, when, and by whom. The worst leaders' response is "If I can't do it, it can't be done." To prevent being overwhelmed leaders must select, train, motivate, reward and **use** people whose abilities supplement their own. When the constant message is, "you are involved only because I can't take the time to do this myself" people are delighted to see an overworked boss fail. When they believe they are likely to be replaced by a machine at the first opportunity, they look for ways to make that decision fail. When they think their best effort is never good enough, they look for ways to make the leader look bad. When they feel unappreciated they find ways for the company to fail.

- **Most of their accomplishments are shallow.**

Otto (Bob) Nottlemann rose to be president of Inland Steel Co., one of the largest in the U.S. When he retired in 1987 he decided to devote his time to non-profit organizations. For nine years, he served as chairman of the Executive Services Corps of Chicago, which organizes former executives to train and help leaders in charities. He also led a drive to raise $1 million for a Service Corps Endowment and was founding chairman of a foundation for his local school district. His motive was simply "to give back what he could."

> The receiver is helped.
> The giver is blessed.

On the other hand, those driven by too much ego are so busy attracting attention to themselves they don't even notice others' needs. The very best examples are the so called leaders who show up to blame somebody every time a TV camera records a tragedy and pretend to "feel the pain" of the victim(s), or the business owner or manager who fake sincere interest in an employee's personal problems. My best advice is Caring Can't Be Faked—If you don't believe it/feel it—don't say it.

- **Their vanity drives away possible supporters.**

The vanity exhibited by extremely forceful individuals sometimes achieves short-term results. Long-term, however, many serious problems arise because:

1. A superhuman effort is required to attempt to provide the answers everyone needs.

2. The "hero complex" wears thin when the inevitable mistakes become obvious.

3. Without sharing in problem ownership there is no sharing of responsibility for solutions.

4. Authenticity is doubted when people see repeated evidence of "me first" behavior. Their conclusion is, "the person needs praise, recognition and getting their way more than they need me, my help or even getting the results the organization needs."

5. When leaders are judged to be self seeking and artificial, everything they ask for is suspect. People don't know whether instructions are addressing actual priorities or personal whims.

6. Problem resolution is limited to what they want rather than what facts reveal.

7. Trust is missing when orders and instructions prevail over investigation, documentation and testing.

- **They won't show appreciation.**

> You're only as good as your last race.
>
> —Jackie Joyner-Kersee
> Olympic and World Record Holder

- **They refuse to be sympathetic.**

A young man named Kurtis was stocking shelves in a grocery store, when he heard the voice of a new cashier over the intercom, calling for help with a carry out. Since Kurtis was almost finished, he answered the call. When he approached the counter, he saw her smile, and realized how beautiful the new cashier was. He fell in love at first sight.

He looked at her punchcard. Her name was Brenda. He noticed she walked home. The next day, he offered her a ride. She accepted. He asked if he might see her again. She said no, it was impossible—she had two children. He offered to pay for a baby-sitter, so she reluctantly said yes. When he arrived at her door, she said she couldn't make it after all, because the sitter had canceled. So Kurtis suggested bringing the kids. She hesitated, but finally invited him inside to meet them.

Her daughter was cute as could be, and then Brenda brought out her young son, in a wheelchair. She explained that he was born paraplegic, with Down Syndrome. Kurtis persisted in asking why the kids couldn't go with them. Brenda was shocked. She thought most men would run from a woman with two kids, especially when one had disabilities. That's what her ex-husband, who fathered them did—but not Kurtis.

That evening, they took the kids to dinner and a movie. When her son needed something, Kurtis was right there. When he needed to use the restroom, Kurtis lifted him, took him and returned him to his wheelchair. Both kids loved him. By the end of that evening, Brenda made up her mind, she wanted to spend the rest of her life with him. One year later, they were married. He adopted both kids, and since then they have had two of their own. Mr. and Mrs. Kurt Warner now live in St. Louis, where he has a job as quarterback with the St. Louis Rams—the Super Bowl winners in 2000. Kurt was the most valuable player.

- **They believe admitting mistakes is a sign of weakness.**

The weakest people in leadership positions hope that their weaknesses will either be undiscovered or ignored. They are wrong on both counts. It also shows disrespect for the intelligence of the people they must work with. Rather than live fearing weaknesses, the key is to capitalize on strengths and work around weaknesses.

Take golfer Tiger Woods for example. His greatest weakness is playing out of sand traps. He ranks 61st among tour professionals in "sand saves." Does that stop him from winning? No way. Woods keeps improving his accuracy and distance so he manages to avoid the sand. In the 1999 British Open, where there were more bunkers than most other places, only one golfer avoided them all—Tiger Woods.

Humble people find it is easier to admit mistakes because:

— they know they will have more credibility over
time
— they believe their critics will not be so harsh if
they are not haughty or try to hide the truth
— they have a chance to get sympathy and help
from some people

— they can move forward quickly from their
mistake and go on to solving problems.

The best advice is to be realistic.

— Don't fool yourself into believing your
weaknesses can be disguised or hidden. Sooner or
later your deceit will be discovered and you will
be worse off.
— Focus on getting better at what you already
do well. Remember: if failing to overcome a
weakness allows strengths to deteriorate, you
suffer a double loss.
— Select people whose strengths cover your
weaknesses so that *together* you can accomplish
what must be done.

Bill Gates, founder of Microsoft, is a visualizer not an
implementer. He acknowledged this by selecting Steve
Ballmer to manage the plans and objectives needed daily
for continuing, profitable growth.

- **Their towering ambition exceeds reality.**

Ambition is undeniably an essential building block for
success. But when it supercedes common sense and requires
being a hero every day, progress decays and good people leave.
The key is to help everyone see where and how they can have
an impact on results achieved. The need is to associate with
people who want to be accountable—who don't need a hero
to protect them from responsibility.

Humble people want to think for themselves. They want
leaders who will ask the right questions, investigate options,
seek involvement, get input, delegate and base rewards on
performance.

Dave Thomas succeeded in winning the hearts and stom-
achs of millions of Americans. The founder of Wendy's—the

third largest hamburger chain in the country—was a smiling, friendly and down-to-earth TV adman for more than 10 years. Many people were saddened by his recent death. He dedicated his life not only to selling great burgers, but to helping those less fortunate. His popularity never went to his head, and he always considered himself "just a hamburger cook."

Being adopted as a baby led him to be an advocate for adoption. He created the Dave Thomas Foundation for Adoption, a non-profit agency to raise public awareness. He testified before Congress encouraging them to create incentives for adoption. "I know firsthand how important it is for every child to have a home and loving family," he said in his testimony, "Without a family, I would not be where I am today."

Thomas actually became a millionaire at 35 years old, buying and selling four failing Kentucky Fried Chicken franchises. He then invested in his own fast-food chain, which started with one restaurant in 1969, and has grown to 6,000 worldwide, with sales topping $8 billion annually. He was in more than 800 Wendy's ads, but kept insisting that he'd quit doing them as soon as they weren't working any more. Obviously, they did.

His rags to riches story earned him the Horatio Alger Award in 1979. Thomas felt fortunate to have been born in the U.S. and believed that only in America could a guy like him become so successful even without a high school diploma. His humble beginnings led to humility throughout his entire life.

11

Closing Thoughts

I have reached the conclusion that humble people can prevail for 3 key reasons:

— They are more appreciative for what they have.
— They are not envious of what others have.
— They are grateful for things most people take for granted.

> An envier not only wants what you have, he wants you not to have it.
>
> —Harriet Rubin, writer

In my own case:

My Cup Runneth Over

Humility can prevail if we
are truly thankful. I am
thankful and need to be
humble because—

1. I am well and can tolerate my pains.
2. I can see, hear, speak and *think*.
3. I am surrounded by loved ones.
4. I have earned the respect of my
   wife and daughters.
5. I have useful work to do.
6. I have many people to thank for
   favors.
7. I have had exemplary people to
   learn from.
8. I can help those in need.
9. My faith overcomes obstacles.
10. I can worship freely.
11. I can speak my mind without fear.
12. I can criticize my government
    without hesitation.
13. I can join any group I choose.
14. I can base my reputation on
    accomplishment not dependence.
15. I can stretch myself to new
    achievements.

How about you?

This outlook of thankfulness tends to crowd out the negative, self-defeating effects of envy. Humble people can ignore the endless power struggles it causes. They can also avoid the even-worse tragedy of having selfishness rule their lives.

Index